KNOW IDEAS

Yet more serious fun for youth groups

Contents

Whatever you do, DO NOT START HERE!

Know Ideas 2! is crammed full of ideas for young people's groups. Unlike most CYFA resources it is not a Bible-based teaching programme. It is not meant to be the starting point for your planning, but a source of extra ideas to help give your programme originality, enjoyment, seriousness, wit, buzz, bite, spice and integrity. Want to use them well? Then...

■ A point to you

The ideas come from many different settings. They were mostly thought up by people who had particular aims in mind. Make sure you know what you want an activity to achieve for you. Then you can adapt, mould, batter, cajole and forge it into your own better version that will help you and your group get to grips with the Bible, have radical Christian relationships and, very occasionally (if you really must), enjoy yourselves.

■ Keep out of the creek

Some of the ideas will help you to look at the Bible with your group. There are icebreakers, games and other starters to lead into looking at the Bible, and good ways to get the group thinking, talking and doing something about its message. Beware of using the ideas as short cuts. You will probably get lost. Do your honest thinking, praying and responding to the Bible first. Then choose ideas which will help you tackle it with the group in the best way.

■ Don't do it

A lot of the activities in the book are specifically designed to help build up relationships: within your group of young people, between leaders and group members, and between the young people and others in the church. Unfortunately, it is easy to lead them in ways that make young people feel embarrassed or inadequate. That is a bad idea. Make sure that the way you lead any activity builds up good relationships too. Be sensitive to the needs of different individuals, including those who are most different from you. Allow individuals space to opt in and opt out, and to take different roles which suit them.

Dare to try something new – and dare not to, sometimes, too! Use a good range of lively, reflective, weird and wild, clever, simple, far-out and far-in ideas which will fit the people in your group. To use new ideas effectively requires some time and effort. *Know Ideas 2!* should make you want to put in the work to try out something new, and to come up with your own ideas, too. But don't start here. In the end, God is more interested in our faithfulness to him and to his young people than in the originality of our group programmes.

1 Fun and Games

Icebreakers and longer games

These ideas can help you to introduce a group session, explore a teaching point or just have fun together. When you use a short game to defrost the group, beware of cracking up. Make sure that it involves people in a way they can cope with, rather than excluding anyone. Icebreakers are fine unless you are the ice! A good icebreaker gets people talking and leads into the theme of the meeting. Longer games too need to help things flow, not freeze.

1 Blow Up

Aim:	*To break the ice and introduce a difficult theme*
Ideal group size:	*Any*
Time needed:	*3-8 minutes*
Equipment needed:	*Identical balloons, bubble gum*

Give out identical balloons to everyone in the group. Tell them that you will give a prize to the person who blows up the biggest balloon without it popping. The prize can be bubble gum so that they can continue to practise blowing! If you are going to be discussing something that group members find difficult later on in the meeting, you could use this as an introduction. Ask them how they felt when they were blowing the balloons up. Were they nervous? Did they push the balloon to the limit, or did they leave it at a safe but rather boring size?

2 Foil Faces

Aim:	*To break the ice and get everyone involved and talking*
Ideal group size:	*5+*
Time needed:	*3-10 minutes*
Equipment needed:	*Kitchen foil, Blu-Tack*

Get the group members to press their faces into pieces of aluminium kitchen foil, to make 3-D masks. Display them on the wall and try to guess who is who.

3 Backward Writing

Aim:	*To break the ice and get group members concentrating*
Ideal group size:	*Up to 10*
Time needed:	*3-5 minutes*
Equipment needed:	*Mirrors, paper, pens*

Bring along a mirror and challenge the group to write their full name and address so that it is clearly readable through the mirror – extra credit for joined-up writing!

4 Violent Coordination Exercise

Aim:	*To break the ice and punch yourselves on the nose*
Ideal group size:	*Any*
Time needed:	*3-5 minutes*
Equipment needed:	*None*

Hold your right ear with your left hand and hold your nose with your right hand. Then drop your hands to the floor and do it again. Drop your hands to the floor, clap your hands on your knees, clap your hands, then do it again. Now swap so that your right hand holds your left ear and left hand your nose. (Still with it?) Repeat the whole process. Alternate doing it the two ways round. Anyone who hasn't punched themselves in the face by the end is too well coordinated by half.

5 Tapehead

Aim:	*To have fun*
Ideal group size:	*4+*
Time needed:	*15 minutes*
Equipment needed:	*Masking tape or Sellotape, selection of light objects*

Select some willing volunteers and put them into pairs. Ask one of each pair to wrap their partner's head, completely, in masking tape or *Sellotape*, with the sticky surface *facing outwards*. (Make sure they can breathe!) Then have a competition by getting the 'mummies' to crawl or run to an area where there is a variety of small light objects spread out. The aim is to get as many items as possible to stick to their heads, return to their partner, who removes the objects, and then return for more! The winners are those with the most objects. Good objects are: egg cartons, polystyrene cups, plastic kitchenware, milk cartons, construction paper, shoe boxes, string, tie pins, rubber bands, marshmallows, etc.

6 Chattered Teeth

Aim:	*To break the ice*
Ideal group size:	*5+*
Time needed:	*5-10 minutes*
Equipment needed:	*Ice-pops or lollies*

This is almost literally an icebreaker! Give everyone in the group an ice-pop or cheap ice lolly and see who can eat it the fastest. This is actually quite painful to do for people with sensitive teeth, so watch out for headaches! If you have a large enough group, split up into teams of equal size and have a relay. To do this, the first person in each team has to eat their ice-pop, and only when they have finished can the next person start on theirs, and so on until the whole team have finished.

7 Paper Chase

Aim:	*To get group members working in groups and to introduce a current issue*
Ideal group size:	*6+*
Time needed:	*10-15 minutes*
Equipment needed:	*Identical newspapers*

Buy several copies of the same newspaper (broadsheets work best for this game) and make a list of headlines from different pages in the paper. Then rearrange the pages of each paper, re-fold and so on, so they are really messed up. Split into groups of three or six and sit each group very close together in two rows, with knees touching. With a three, sit them in a triangle with knees touching. Give each group a mixed-up newspaper and see who can rearrange it correctly fastest. Follow this up by reading out a headline and see which group can shout out the page number first. If the group is sensible they will distribute the pages amongst the group.

8 Finger Grab

Aim:	*To break the ice or to introduce working in pairs*
Ideal group size:	*4+*
Time needed:	*3-5 minutes*
Equipment needed:	*None*

Divide into pairs and then give out these instructions:
Face your partner. Hold out your left hand, palm up. Now place the index finger of your right hand into your partner's palm so it just touches, pointing downwards. On the command 'go' try to grab your partner's index finger whilst avoiding having your own finger grabbed.

Play the best of three. It could turn into a knock-out competition or World Championship if someone doesn't put a stop to it.

9 Group Sort

Aim:	*To get group members working together and to introduce new group members*
Ideal group size:	*5+*
Time needed:	*5-10 minutes*
Equipment needed:	*None*

Get the group to arrange themselves into a line in various orders. Try: age, height, alphabetical order of Christian names, numbers of letters in whole name, length of end thumb joint. To add to the pressure you could do it in two teams. This is good for learning names and getting people moving round and interacting. You could choose attributes which fit with your theme.

10 Banana Duel

Aim:	*To get group members working in pairs and to make a mess*
Ideal group size:	*4+*
Time needed:	*15 minutes*
Equipment needed:	*Bananas, string, blindfolds (optional), towels*

Team up the contestants in pairs and ask them to clasp their left hands together. Now tie these hands firmly. Give each player a banana with the following instructions:

1. Peel the banana in any way you can (usually with teeth and free hands).
2. Once peeled, try to cram the whole banana into your partner's mouth.
3. The winner is the first person to complete stages 1 and 2.

Handy hints:
- ❑ squashy bananas work best
- ❑ you could blindfold the pairs
- ❑ you could have a banana duel tag match in teams
- ❑ what about chocolate sauce?

11 What's the Word?

Aim:	*To get the whole group concentrating and listening to each other or to introduce the theme*
Ideal group size:	*5+*
Time needed:	*5-10 minutes*
Equipment needed:	*Pen, paper, water (optional)*

Sit in a circle. Someone is 'on'. They choose a subject such as 'the kitchen' and a secret key word which they write down, such as 'spoons'. Go round the group saying words connected to the subject. If anyone says the key word they are then 'on'. Alternatively choose subjects yourself, all linked to your theme for the meeting. Add to the tension by throwing a glass of water in the face of the unlucky victim (if the meeting room can cope with it).

12 Uniped

Aim:	*To get group members working together and as a lead in to working in groups*
Ideal group size:	*8+*
Time needed:	*3-5 minutes*
Equipment needed:	*None*

If your group is large, for this activity you will need to split into equally sized smaller groups, each with eight to fifteen people. Each group has to develop a strategy (and carry it out!) by which they can lift the entire group off the floor, having as few legs or other limbs as possible touching the floor. The group must be able to support itself for at least ten seconds! If you have more than one group they can compete against each other. Otherwise the group could set records for itself to break on other occasions.

13 Zoom, Boing, Splat, Wah, Eek!

Aim:	*To get group members concentrating and to create confusion*
Ideal group size:	*6+*
Time needed:	*5-10 minutes*
Equipment needed:	*None*

Sit in a circle. The first person turns to a neighbour and says 'zoom'. The neighbour then turns to the next person and does likewise. Go right round the circle.

Introduce 'boing'. If someone says 'boing' then they must say so to the face of the person who 'zoomed' at them. The direction is thus changed. Everyone now has a choice as to whether they 'boing' or 'zoom'.

Confusion mounts as you introduce, one by one:

- 'splat' – this changes direction with you looking the opposite way, like something 'splatting' into the back of your head
- 'wah' – this doesn't change direction, but you must look the opposite way
- 'eek' – this is like a 'zoom' but misses out one person.

Regional variations are possible; confusion reigns. Try to have a group record for keeping it going without error.

14 Double Bed

Aim:	*To get group members working together*
Ideal group size:	*4+*
Time needed:	*10 minutes*
Equipment needed:	*One old mattress*

Work in groups of about eight for a double mattress, four for a single. The object of the game is for the whole group, standing on the mattress, to turn it over without touching the floor. This game doesn't have to be competitive, just fun, but make it a race against the clock if you want. Have a camera handy.

15 Balloon Stomp

Aim:	*To get group members working together and as a lead in to working in groups*
Ideal group size:	*4+*
Time needed:	*3-10 minutes*
Equipment needed:	*A lot of coloured balloons*

Divide the group into teams of equal numbers and assign a different colour to each team. Then give each team the same number of balloons of their colour. For example, give the red team ten red balloons. Get the teams to blow up all their balloons. When this is done the game begins by releasing all the balloons on to the floor. The object of the game is to pop all the balloons belonging to other teams while protecting your own. You can impose a time limit and the team with most balloons left wins. Alternatively, you can let it be a fight to the last balloon.

16 Handicap Table Tennis

Aim:	*To have fun playing table tennis without the best players dominating*
Ideal group size:	*4+*
Time needed:	*15-45 minutes*
Equipment needed:	*Table tennis equipment, items for handicaps*

You probably know who the best table tennis players are in your group, so create a handicap system. Give each person a handicap, but give the hardest ones to the best players. Beware of labelling some members as 'less good' as they may be hurt by this. Alternatively, write all the handicaps on cards, and get each player to draw one at random before each game. Shorter games (to seven or eleven points) may work best, if you are doing this. You could try some of the following handicaps:

- ❑ play with a frying pan (non-stick)
- ❑ play with an eye patch
- ❑ play with the wrong hand
- ❑ turn through 360 degrees between shots
- ❑ face away from the play and only turn round when you hear the ball hit the table
- ❑ play in a heavy overcoat and wellington boots
- ❑ talk constantly throughout each rally, without hesitation, on a subject of the opponent's choice
- ❑ use a piece of string as a higher net for one player.

17 Gourmet Quiz!

Aim:	*To introduce or revise a theme*
Ideal group size:	*10+*
Time needed:	*5-10 minutes*
Equipment needed:	*Doughnuts and packets of crisps, pen and card for noughts and crosses*

Draw a large noughts and crosses board on the floor or a large piece of card, and number the squares from one to nine. Place one doughnut and one packet of crisps in each square. You will need two sets of questions, each numbered one to nine, perhaps about recent teaching topics, church sermons or things which have happened in the group.

Divide into two teams: the 'doughnuts' and the 'crisps'. In turn, the teams choose one of the numbered squares, and are asked the relevant question. If they answer correctly they get to eat their food from that square. (This could be the whole team or just the person who answered.) Continue like this, but absolutely forbid speaking with food in the mouth. The winning team is the first to eat all the doughnuts (or crisps) in a straight line.

With a large group, have extra questions, doughnuts and crisps, and play it more than once.

18 Tennis Ball Chicken

Aim:	*To break the ice or introduce a session on fear/peer pressure*
Ideal group size:	*5+*
Time needed:	*3-5 minutes*
Equipment needed:	*One tennis ball*

A game for outdoors. Stand in a bunch. The object of the game is not to be distracted by the possibility of something painful being about to happen. Throw a tennis ball up in the air about five metres above the bunch. Everyone should try to stand perfectly still and looking to the front as the ball falls. Anyone moving is out.

19 Frozen Bubbles

Aim:	*To have fun*
Ideal group size:	*Any*
Time needed:	*3-10 minutes*
Equipment needed:	*Bubble solution and wire loops (bought or home-made), bubble gum*

On a cold, clear moonlit night, old-fashioned bubble-blowing is a whole new experience: the bubbles freeze! If the moon does not cooperate, use a torch to add that extra sparkle. To make your own bubble solution, mix water, detergent, food colouring and a small amount of syrup. If you do this you will also need to make wire loops. Get group members to dress up warm – then the possibilities are endless: the biggest, smallest, longest-lasting bubbles all deserve prizes (bubble gum, of course!).

20 Cartoons

Aim:	*To have fun and to get group members thinking creatively*
Ideal group size:	*Any*
Time needed:	*5-10 minutes*
Equipment needed:	*Newspaper and magazine cartoons*

Cut out some cartoons from newspapers or magazines – the larger the better – and leave off the captions. Stick them up on large pieces of paper and put them around the room. Encourage the group to circulate and write their own captions underneath each picture. This is a good activity to have going on during a general coffee and chatting time.

21 My Aunt Likes

Aim:	*To annoy people*
Ideal group size:	*Any*
Time needed:	*Anything from 1 minute to all evening*
Equipment needed:	*None*

This is one of those horrible, lateral thinking games. Tell the group some things that your aunt likes, for instance: 'My aunt likes eels, but hates snakes', or 'My aunt likes knees, but hates elbows'. In short, your aunt likes any item that contains a repeated letter, like 'Russia', 'tomorrow' or 'athlete's foot', and hates any word that does not. Encourage group members to suggest items which your aunt might like and tell them whether they are right. As some of them work it out, they can join in suggesting pairs of items that she likes and dislikes, to the annoyance of the others.

22 Parachute Kickball

Aim:	*To have fun outdoors*
Ideal group size:	*16+*
Time needed:	*30 minutes*
Equipment needed:	*Parachute canopy or large sheet, footballs, four markers*

1. Mark out a 30 metre square with stumps or other markers at each corner.
2. Divide into two teams.
3. Appoint an impartial judge.
4. Team A stands inside the square, holding the parachute or large sheet between them. Team B stands outside the square.
5. Team B kicks a ball into the square using a high, arching goalie kick as seen on all the world's worst football matches.
6. Team A must try to catch the ball in the sheet or parachute for which they score one point. If the ball lands inside the square but not in the sheet then Team B scores one point.
7. After three balls have been caught, Teams A and B swap over. Finish the game before disenchantment with the referee, or physical violence sets in!
8. Why not use two or three balls at once? Or challenge another group to a game with refreshments afterwards – a good relationship builder.

23 Create a Game

Aim:	*To get group members working creatively together and to invent ideas for Know Ideas 3!*
Ideal group size:	*6+*
Time needed:	*15-60 minutes*
Equipment needed:	*A variety of household items and games equipment*

Divide into teams. Give a selection of household items and games equipment to each team: the sillier the better. For example: a mop, a hose, a book, paper clips, balls of different kinds, a telephone directory, paper and pens, and so on. Allow them about seven minutes to create a new sport using as many of their items as possible. Then get each team to demonstrate their game. The rest of the group could award points for originality, workability and stupidity. If you have time, stage a contest with the new games. One of them might become a new favourite for the group.

24 Banana Pass

Aim:	*To break the ice and introduce a session on image/masks*
Ideal group size:	*5+*
Time needed:	*5-10 minutes*
Equipment needed:	*Inflatable banana or other large object, music, sack containing old clothes (preferably garish and unfashionable)*

The game runs along similar lines to 'pass the parcel'. The difference is that instead of a parcel, the banana is passed around the circle. When the music stops the person holding the banana has to put on one of the items of clothing from the sack, which should be placed in the middle of the circle.

25 Askitattack

Aim:	*To have fun and to get people working together in teams*
Ideal group size:	*8+ depending on size of room*
Time needed:	*10-20 minutes*
Equipment needed:	*Two sets of skittles, soft balls*

This is a game for two teams of four or five players, and needs quite a bit of room. Split the room in half, with each team allocated one half, which they must not leave. At each end of the room set up ten skittles, or other suitable objects that can be knocked down. The basic idea is for each team to knock down the other's skittles, whilst defending their own. Use two soft balls to speed the game up. If you have a large enough room, your teams could be larger and more balls could be used.

26 Indoor Olympics

Aim:	*To have fun together*
Ideal group size:	*8+*
Time needed:	*15-60 minutes*
Equipment needed:	*Depends on games planned*

Hold a competition with indoor equivalents of Olympic sports. For example, you could try the following:

- the feather putt – who can throw the feather the furthest?
- javelin – made by joining two straws together
- long jump – from a standing start
- 'heel to toe' marathon
- blow-football in teams.

27 Obstacle Table Tennis

Aim:	*To have fun playing table tennis without the best players dominating*
Ideal group size:	*2+*
Time needed:	*30 minutes – 3 days*
Equipment needed:	*Table tennis equipment, six items to act as obstacles*

This can become compulsive. Groups love it or hate it. It is a great equalizer for those with table tennis skills. Set up table tennis, as normal, but place three everyday items on the table on either side of the net. Don't choose things that may damage a nice table's playing surface. Good obstacles are:

- another bat
- a scarf
- a book
- a small stool or chair
- a set of keys
- a shoe
- a packet of sweets (the winner could keep this).

Play normal table tennis with alternate serves. The obstacles count as part of the table, so you can play on after an obstacle has been hit, if you are clever enough. Each time you win a point you also win an obstacle, of your opponent's choice. The opponent places it wherever they want to, on your side of the table. The winner is the first person to win all six obstacles and a further point.

This works well as a knock-out competition, running alongside a winter games night programme.

28 Torch Hockey

Aim:	*To have fun without getting injured*
Ideal group size:	*8+*
Time needed:	*15 minutes*
Equipment needed:	*Indoor hockey set (preferably improvised), two identical torches*

This version of indoor hockey requires a dark room. It is best with improvised equipment such as rolled-up newspapers and a soft ball, to avoid damaging anyone. The game is identical to indoor hockey, with one difference – the lights are turned out. Each team elects one member to stand against the wall in the opposing team's half, holding a torch. The torches are the only illumination allowed. Make sure you remove any potentially life-threatening objects from the room.

2 Bible Basics

Activities to help your group handle the Bible well

These are ideas which aim to sharpen up the way group members view and handle the Bible. They assume that the Bible has a sharp cutting edge, so it needs to be used with care or there will be a lot of mess. Some of the activities focus on what the Bible is and how to use it; others are methods to use with whatever Bible material you are looking at with young people.

1 When in Rome

Aim:	*To look at Bible passages in their cultural setting*
Ideal group size:	*Any*
Time needed:	*5-20 minutes*
Equipment needed:	*Bibles, appropriate food, clothes, etc.*

Set the scene for looking at a Bible passage by getting into the culture of the day. For example, if you are looking at Romans, use reference books (such as Bible dictionaries, library books or *Asterix the Gaul*) to find out about life in ancient Rome. Then prepare some Roman food and entertainment; ask the members of the group to think of Roman names for themselves for the evening; suggest they come dressed as Romans. The leaders could act as slaves. Announce that you have just received a letter, and read edited highlights of Paul's letter to Rome – possibly the beginning, ending and one particular passage. Follow it up by studying the passage at your next meeting. Was it just a letter for the Romans or is it for us, too?

You could take a similar approach with other New Testament letters, Revelation (find out about one of the seven churches), or Old Testament settings such as the exile in Babylon.

2 Say It with Flowers

Aim:	*To lead into looking at a biblical picture*
Ideal group size:	*Any*
Time needed:	*10 minutes*
Equipment needed:	*Appropriate objects, Bibles*

This method can help if you are looking at a Bible passage which uses an object to make a teaching point. If, for example, you are studying Matthew 6:25-34, where Jesus uses flowers as an example, put a flower or plant in the centre of the group (or have one per small group). Then ask for the most facts about it that anyone can write down in a given time limit. They must all be positive statements, i.e. 'It is…', rather than 'It is not…' When the time is up, go round the group reading out one fact at a time in quick succession; no fact may be repeated. Then lead into your Bible study.

3 All in the Mind

Aim:	*To memorize part of the Bible*
Ideal group size:	*Any*
Time needed:	*Several weeks*
Equipment needed:	*Bibles*

Agree as a group to memorize a Bible passage on the theme you are dealing with. Make it long enough to be a challenge that will take several weeks to achieve, rather than just one or two verses. Encourage them to practise saying it in a way that makes the meaning come across.

4 In the Right Place

Aim:	*To help the setting of Bible passages to come alive*
Ideal group size:	*Any*
Time needed:	*15 minutes – whole meeting*
Equipment needed:	*Bibles, transport*

Hold your meeting in a different place which reflects the passage you are looking at. If there is somewhere local which is appropriate you could just go there to read the passage. For example, if you are looking at Psalm 23, meet in a sheep pasture; for a passage written from or about a jail, see if you can use a local police cell; for the wise and foolish builders or the building of the temple, go to a building site. The possibilities are endless. You will need to get necessary permission or make appropriate arrangements. Only do this occasionally, or decide to do a series together such as 'On the Spot Parables'.

5 Photo Story

Aim:	*To take a fresh look at a Bible narrative*
Ideal group size:	*4+*
Time needed:	*30-60 minutes*
Equipment needed:	*Cameras, film, appropriate props, Bibles*

Get the group members to produce a photo story to illustrate a Bible passage. To do this they will need to plan a sequence of photographs which are needed. Some of the group can then be the actors in the scenes, while others take the photographs. If you can get hold of an instant Polaroid-type camera, so much the better. This can be done on as large or as small a scale as you want. Other people might design and research locations, direct the photography, write captions or mount the pictures for a display, or the same people could do all these.

A slightly simpler but even more hilarious alternative is to bring to the meeting a pile of magazines, colour supplements and the like. Get everyone to plunder these for pictures from which a photo story of the Bible passage can be constructed. As before, get captions written and mount the pictures.

6 Guiding Light

Aim:	*To explore the picture of God's word as light*
Ideal group size:	*Any*
Time needed:	*10 minutes*
Equipment needed:	*Paper, scissors, blindfolds*

Use this idea to introduce Psalm 119:105, 'Your word is a lamp to guide me and a light for my path.' Give everyone a sheet of paper and a pair of scissors. Tell them that they are going to have to cut out the shape of a camel in the dark! If you can effectively black out the room, do so. Otherwise blindfold everybody and turn off the lights as well to prevent cheating. If you do not have enough pairs of scissors, make it more difficult by asking group members to tear out the camel shape.

7 Snowball Study

Aim:	*To study the Bible with the whole group participating*
Ideal group size:	*8+*
Time needed:	*30 minutes*
Equipment needed:	*Bibles*

If your Bible studies consist of expanses of silence while everyone stares at the passage (or the floor, or the ceiling), followed eventually by the inevitable 'Sorry, what was the question again?' then here's a suggestion you might try. After you have read the whole passage through, split it into eight sections each of which makes sense. Give each person in the group just one of the sections to look at and think about. Then put the ones into pairs, so they can each share with the other what they think their section says, and what it means, then put the pairs into fours and get each person to share with the group what their partner has just told them. Finally put the fours into one or more eights and lead gently into a discussion of the whole passage.

Alternatively, you could begin with eight separate, short passages from different parts of the Bible which relate to the single theme you are studying.

8 Drama Build-up

Aim:	*To explore a Bible passage through drama*
Ideal group size:	*Any*
Time needed:	*30 minutes*
Equipment needed:	*None*

This method helps group members to explore the people involved in a Bible passage, in a way that builds up gradually. It is very good for unfamiliar bits of Old Testament narrative. (The examples are for the account of the fall of Jericho in Joshua 5:13 – 6:27.)

- ❑ Begin by calling out some feelings which are shown by people in the Bible passage: shocked, confident, terrified, etc. Each person must make their face show each feeling as you say it. Do the feelings in the order they appear in the narrative.
- ❑ Go through the same feelings again, but this time ask everyone to show them with their whole bodies, including their faces. Instead of just 'terrified', fill out the detail of the story a tiny bit: 'shocked at meeting an angel', 'confident about a plan of action', 'terrified of an enemy', etc.
- ❑ This time, try out a series of mime actions from the story. Practise each one together, working out how it might be shown clearly: 'realizing someone you are talking to is an angel', 'taking off your shoes', 'locking gates against an enemy', etc.
- ❑ Finally tell the whole story, or read it out from the Bible. Pause at the most dramatic points for everyone to get themselves into a frozen picture of that moment in the story, using the feelings and actions you practised.

Afterwards, use the ideas that have come out of this to lead into looking at the teaching of the Bible passage.

9 Conflict Drama

Aim:	*To help group members to apply what they are learning to themselves*
Ideal group size:	*3+*
Time needed:	*30-45 minutes*
Equipment needed:	*None*

Use this idea after looking at a Bible passage, when you have already agreed on the basic principle(s) that the Bible passage is teaching. Work in small groups. Allow just five minutes for each group to imagine a conflict situation where someone is trying to obey that truth, but where they are being tempted to ignore or compromise it. It should be an everyday situation.

Then give the groups five more minutes to improvise a dramatic sketch of that situation with a beginning, a middle (the actual conflict) and an end which resolves the conflict or, better, leaves the dilemma clearly stated.

Giving young people the freedom, within these fairly tight time constraints, to apply the Bible like that will often produce ideas that would not otherwise have surfaced. When they perform the sketches for each other, allow the discussion to roam free by asking pertinent questions: 'Why did you decide to end it like that?', 'Why do you think Tom said what he did?', 'Was that what you would have done? Why?' etc.

10 A Good Likeness

Aim:	*To introduce biblical pictures of God's word*
Ideal group size:	*5+*
Time needed:	*10 minutes*
Equipment needed:	*Selection of objects*

Collect together a wide variety of objects – a wellington boot, a ping-pong ball, a toy car, a banana – the odder the better, one for each member. Split into groups of about six. Place in the centre of each group as many objects as there are group members. Get the group to number themselves and then tell them that number three will go first. Each person has to pick up one of the objects and say 'I am like a... because...' For example, 'I am like a welly because I'm always putting my foot in it.' After someone has chosen an object they keep hold of it so that no one else can choose it. Continue round the group until everyone has had a go. The last person won't have any choice of object.

Next, choose a category (e.g. a named pop group, Aston Villa, the group leader, our singing), and ask each group to decide which of their objects is like this category, and why. Do several of these before asking the groups to choose a category for 'The Bible is like... because...' Then look at what the Bible says the word of God is like, for example:

- ❑ bread — Deuteronomy 8:3
- ❑ a light — Psalm 119:105
- ❑ rain — Isaiah 55:10-11
- ❑ fire — Jeremiah 20:9
- ❑ a sword — Ephesians 6:17; Hebrews 4:12.

Discuss why these pictures are used, and whether they should make any difference to the way we use the Bible.

11 God's Word

Aim:	*To introduce some teaching on the Bible*
Ideal group size:	*Any*
Time needed:	*20 minutes*
Equipment needed:	*Bibles, pens, paper*

Psalm 119 has a great deal to say about the word of God and especially about God's instruction for us. Split up into small groups to scour this psalm for what it says about God's word to us. Have different people or groups looking out for:

- ❑ different words used to refer to God's word
- ❑ pictures of what God's word is like
- ❑ descriptions of what God's word does.

When each group has its list, or after a time limit, they should then write down what each of the things they have found tells us about God and his word. Then have the groups report back.

12 In a Word

Aim:	*To think what it means to talk about God's 'word'*
Ideal group size:	*Any*
Time needed:	*5-10 minutes*
Equipment needed:	*Pens and paper*

Try some word association. Give the group pens and paper. They must all put the pens down and close their eyes. Tell them that you are going to say one word. When they hear it they must open their eyes and write down the first single word that comes into their head. Try BLACK, SPEAK, FIRE, BOX, SMELL, etc. Discuss (without directing too much) whether we can learn anything about words from this exercise. Suggestions might be that words are powerful; they make us think of things; words have different effects on different hearers. Discuss whether those ideas shed any light on what it means to call the Bible 'God's word'.

13 Jabber

Aim:	*To start discussion about taking notice of the Bible*
Ideal group size:	*Any*
Time needed:	*20 minutes*
Equipment needed:	*Pre-recorded tape*

Use a tape recorder to record several people talking at once. These should not be group members. Each one must read out or talk about something different, e.g. a story, a recipe, a newspaper, a nursery rhyme, sing a song. One should read a well-known Bible passage. Play the tape to the group and ask them to identify as many of the things recorded on it as they can.

Discuss the question 'Which do I take most notice of, my friends, the Bible or the TV – when deciding on what to wear, when planning how to spend Sundays, when choosing what to pray about, when thinking about my future?'

14 Writereading

Aim:	*To provoke discussion about how we read and understand different types of literature in the Bible*
Ideal group size:	*Any*
Time needed:	*10 minutes*
Equipment needed:	*Highway code, other pieces of writing*

Read part of the Highway Code out loud to the group as if you were reading poetry. Continue the pretence by asking the group questions such as 'How did it make you feel?' and go on to note the poet's clever use of alliteration, and the underlying logic provided by the persistent 'car-motif' (or that sort of thing). Use this to start discussion about what happens when bits of the Bible are not taken in context. How can we make sure we ask the right sort of questions about different parts of the Bible?

This could be made into a group activity by giving small groups different books/pieces of writing with the wrong sort of questions to answer on them, e.g. a comic with questions like: 'What can we learn from this about how to keep pets?' or a dictionary with 'What is the author trying to teach us about life?'

15 Childlike

Aim:	*To provoke discussion about reading Bible passages in context*
Ideal group size:	*Any*
Time needed:	*20 minutes*
Equipment needed:	*Cards with questions on*

Prepare a set of cards each with one of the following questions written on it: 'What should I buy at the shops tomorrow?', 'Who should I be friends with?', 'What shall I have for dinner on Thursday?', 'What sort of job should I try to get?', 'Should I always obey my parents?' Add more questions so that you have one for each member of the group, or one per small group of two or three.

Announce that you are going to use the Bible to find the answers to these questions. Open your Bible at random, stick your finger somewhere on the page, and read out Matthew 18:3 (memorize it beforehand or make sure the Bible opens on the right page). Each member or small group has to decide what they would do if that is the answer to their question.

Ask the group what question Matthew 18:3 really was the answer to. Do we ever treat the Bible as a lottery? Can the Bible help us answer the sort of questions on the cards? If yes, how? If no, how do we decide what to do in our everyday lives?

16 Read Out

Aim:	*To help group members read the Bible out loud*
Ideal group size:	*Any*
Time needed:	*30-90 minutes*
Equipment needed:	*Bibles*

Run a workshop either as a one-off event for anyone interested, or as part of a session on using the Bible. You could offer alternatives such as 'act out' (using drama to explore the Bible) and 'shout out' (using the Bible in praise). Ask any interested members if they would be willing to read the Bible in church. If you know someone who is dramatically minded they may be able to help you.

17 Read the Gospel

Aim:	*To hear the Bible 'as it is'*
Ideal group size:	*Any*
Time needed:	*2 hours*
Equipment needed:	*Bibles, refreshments*

One of the easiest evening sessions to prepare is to read a whole Gospel through. The CYFA group in Chester-le-Street, County Durham, did it and it took about one-and-a-half hours to read Mark's Gospel. They took a break for chips after Mark 8:29a 'Who do you say that I am?'

It is good to programme in a break, perhaps for food. Then you can advertise 'Mark and Mars Bars', or 'John and Jam Sandwiches', 'Curried Corinthians', etc. (Yes, we know Corinthians isn't a Gospel.)

For extra atmosphere do it with appropriate background music, or read from *The Dramatized Bible* where appropriate. Dim the lights and use candles if you can.

3 BRAIN STARTERS

Active methods to get your group thinking and discussing

The ideas in this chapter are general methods which can be used with whatever Bible material or theme you are looking at. Many are interesting ways to get a discussion started. Discussion can be an 'Oh no, not again' part of your programme, or a setting for young people to try out ideas, wrestle with the truth and learn from each other. Re-using a technique which your group members like can be helpful, but avoid over-use of any one method.

1 Alternate Words

Aim:	*To give an attention-grabbing introduction to a theme*
Ideal group size:	*Any*
Time needed:	*5 minutes*
Equipment needed:	*None*

Get a couple of group members to improvize an introduction to the main theme of the evening, using one word each, alternately.

2 Musical Meanings

Aim:	*To introduce a theme*
Ideal group size:	*Any*
Time needed:	*10 minutes*
Equipment needed:	*Cassette/CD and player, pens and paper*

Listen to all the current top 40, or the sort of music that your group are into. Try to find a song that might illustrate or relate to something about your theme. Have the song playing as your group come in at the start of the session, and get them to write down what they think it means. Share your ideas, then broaden the discussion on to the desired topic. The following songs are not in the charts any more, but worked well in their time, and show the sort of idea. You will be able to find loads of links with current songs, with a bit of lateral thinking!

- ❑ Phil Collins – 'Find a way to my heart' (prayer)
- ❑ Stevie Wonder – 'Skeletons' (guilt/conscience)
- ❑ Steve Camp – 'Whatever you ask' (servanthood)
- ❑ Tears for Fears – 'Sowing the seeds of love' (love)
- ❑ Elton John – 'Healing hands' (caring for each other)

3 Flickstart

Aim:	*To introduce a theme and provoke discussion*
Ideal group size:	*Any*
Time needed:	*2 hours*
Equipment needed:	*VCR, TV and videotape, or cinema tickets and transport*

Why not try using a currently popular film to spark off discussion on issues relating to the Christian life? You could either hire a video or go, as a group, to the local cinema to see a film. The video has the advantage of your being able to show selected snatches for discussion there and then. The cinema trip has the additional bonus of being a good group event in itself.

Always try to watch the film yourself beforehand, so that you can prepare some feeder questions for discussion (this will be easy if you are using a video). A couple of suggestions would be to use *The Mission* to prompt discussion on denominational differences, different approaches to the outworkings of faith, and the use of violence in one's cause; *Letter to Brezhnev* could be used as an introduction to studies on love and sex.

Be very sensitive to the film's classification and the possible attitude of parents of your group members.

4 On the Line

Aim:	*To start discussion and to get everyone expressing their views*
Ideal group size:	*Any*
Time needed:	*10 minutes*
Equipment needed:	*Chair, string, clothes pegs*

Sit the group in a circle with a chair in the centre. Each member holds a piece of string, the other end of which is tied to the chair. They also have a supply of clothes pegs. You read out a statement and if they agree with it strongly, they put a peg at the chair end of their string. If they strongly disagree they must put it at the end of the string that they are holding. They may also put it anywhere along the string between the two. Choose statements that will provoke different reactions, for example 'Parents should be obeyed'. This method can be used to look at attitudes to almost anything: parents, sex, belief, the Bible, ambitions.

The pegs could be numbered beforehand and strings compared at the end to lead into further study of the topic.

5 Collage

Aim:	*To explore a theme creatively and to start discussion*
Ideal group size:	*4+*
Time needed:	*30 minutes*
Equipment needed:	*Pieces of card, old magazines, glue, scissors*

This is a very old idea but is usually fun. Have a supply of old colour magazines, glue, card and scissors. Give the group a subject (e.g. 'the church', 'society', 'school') and ask them to cut out pictures and words which illustrate their views on the subject. They can then stick them on a piece of card to make a small collage. Debrief by discussing each collage in turn. This leads well into a Bible study on the subject. You could display the finished collages.

6 Telemessage

Aim:	*To introduce a theme or to sum up what has been learned*
Ideal group size:	*Any*
Time needed:	*10 minutes*
Equipment needed:	*Pens, paper or telemessage forms*

Tell the group that they are each going to send someone a message relating to your theme. For example, it might be about Jesus. Unfortunately you can only afford telemessages fifteen words long. Each member has to decide what they think is the most important message about Jesus and fit it into fifteen words. Take it in turns to read the messages and say why they put what they did. You could produce your own telemessage forms with spaces for fifteen words for the group to fill in.

Other examples of telemessages which might fit in with different themes are: 'Explain what you do in a typical day'; 'What have you learned in this meeting?'

7 Communal Poetry

Aim:	*To start discussion on a theme*
Ideal group size:	*4+*
Time needed:	*10-15 minutes*
Equipment needed:	*Paper, pens*

Sit in a circle. Give the group a theme for a poem. Each person has to think up and write down the first line of a poem on that theme. They then have to pass their piece of paper to the person on their left, who has to write the next line to continue the poem they are now holding. The poems do not have to rhyme. Continue like this until they get back to the beginning. Read out some of the results.

8 Mastermind

Aim:	*To get group members thinking about the theme beforehand and to start discussion*
Ideal group size:	*4+*
Time needed:	*10-30 minutes*
Equipment needed:	*Subject cards, black chair and spotlight (optional)*

Whatever your subject, the week before the meeting give each group member a card with a related idea or Bible passage, and ask them to go away and think about it. Tell them no more than that! On the night of the study, arrange the chairs in a circle, with one chair, preferably of the black swivel variety, in the middle. Once all are seated, have group members sit in the chair, one by one, and read out their cards. Then ask them to say some of their own thoughts on that subject. The group could then question them, or have an open discussion. Don't ask all the group, but keep them guessing as to who is the next. Be careful not to embarrass those who would not like this: allow them to say 'no' easily, but go as far as you know your group are comfortable with. You could even have the spotlight, music, and 'Your chosen subject is…'

9 Voxpop

Aim:	*To help group members express their views*
Ideal group size:	*Any*
Time needed:	*10 minutes*
Equipment needed:	*Camcorder, VCR, videotape*

Use a video camera to interview some or all of your group members before the meeting, then play it back at some relevant point. A good method is to get them all to give brief answers to the same question. The same method can be used with an audio tape recorder.

Group members could also use this technique to get the views of different church members or others, for use in a group session. Be sensitive to those who don't want to be interviewed – not all people like seeing themselves on video!

10 Focus

Aim:	*To help the group reflect and pray at the start of a meeting*
Ideal group size:	*Any*
Time needed:	*5 minutes*
Equipment needed:	*Bible*

Often leaders come to the group meeting exhausted after a busy day and members come in very high spirits. To allow time to quieten down and focus on the true purpose of meeting together, it may be good, sometimes, to start the meeting by reading a psalm, or other appropriate passage from the Bible. People can then spend a short time thinking about the passage in silence. This can easily lead into a time of introductory prayer.

11 Before and After

Aim:	*To start a discussion or to reflect and sum up what has been learned*
Ideal group size:	*Any*
Time needed:	*5-15 minutes*
Equipment needed:	*Paper and pens*

Work in small groups to prepare adverts for some product that you have given them, e.g. 'WonderMog Cat Food'. Give each group a different product. Each must show the change that product will make to the user. The adverts can be in any form – drama (TV/radio), a poster, a salesman's script, etc.

Then make up adverts for prayer (or whatever your theme is), again showing the difference it makes to people. Lead into discussion, or use it at the end of the session to sum up what you have done.

12 Answer Back

Aim:	*To find out members' views at the end of a meeting and to link between meetings*
Ideal group size:	*10+*
Time needed:	*5-10 minutes*
Equipment needed:	*Questionnaires, pens*

Finish the meeting by handing round a questionnaire to do with the theme you are looking at. Analyze the results and present them at the start of the next meeting. Multiple-choice style questions are the easiest to use as you can count up the number of people who have given each possible answer for each question.

13 Tickertape

Aim:	*To help group members explore issues and priorities*
Ideal group size:	*6+*
Time needed:	*30-60 minutes*
Equipment needed:	*Series of news bulletins, paper, pens, glue, adverts, pictures*

This activity requires some preparation, but can help group members to explore issues in some depth and to create mayhem in the process. You need to invent six different news stories and, for each one, prepare before the meeting a series of bulletins which give progressively more information about the stories. They should all become more interesting as greater sensations 'break'. If possible, type the bulletins.

Divide into groups of three to four, and give each group the real or made-up title of a different daily paper and a rough idea of whether it is to be sensationalist, hyper-intellectual, or whatever. Also provide each group with paper, pens, glue, adverts, pictures, etc., and one piece of paper large enough to be the front page of their newspaper. Set a time deadline by which they must come up with a complete front page. Then hand out three bulletins about different stories so they can begin work.

As the activity progresses, hand out the later bulletins to all the groups. Some should be about new stories, some update previous ones, and some contradict previous reports. Each group must select which items to include on their front page and rewrite them as appropriate. They can also add anything else to the front page in the way of adverts, pictures, etc. Keep the bulletins coming just fast enough to keep the groups busy, and towards the print deadline just a bit too fast, with more of the reports now contradicting earlier ones.

Possible newspaper titles would be: *Daily Blunder*; *Insight*; *Daily Slush*; *The Truth*. Alternatively, let the groups choose their own titles.

You could include items relating to any theme or issue you want to introduce. Alternatively, make the stories biblical and afterwards look at a theme such as 'How reliable are the Gospels?'

14 Memo

Aim:	*To reflect on and apply what has been learned*
Ideal group size:	*Any*
Time needed:	*5 minutes*
Equipment needed:	*Pens, memo sheets, envelopes*

At the end of a Bible study, talk or discussion give out envelopes and sheets of paper, blank except for 'Memo to me' which you have written or photocopied on each. Ask everyone to write themselves a private note beginning: 'The main thing that God has taught me tonight is…' Then ask them to write: 'What I need to do about it this week is…' Ask them to seal the note up in the envelope with their name on the front. Give these out next week. When they have read their own note silently, have a time of prayer. Make sure the leaders take part in this exercise, too.

15 Two Cards

Aim:	*To give everyone the opportunity to contribute to a discussion*
Ideal group size:	*4+*
Time needed:	*5-15 minutes*
Equipment needed:	*Cards*

Use this to even out the contributions to a discussion from those who are normally over-eloquent and those who are totally silent. Hand each member two cards at the start. They should write their names on these cards. Explain that when anyone wants to make a comment they must hand in a card to whoever is in the chair (yourself or an independent third party). Once they have handed in their cards, they may not speak again. The only person who is able to speak is the one whose card is 'in play'. The chairman's decision is final. You may want to allow some questions that do not require cards – for example, asking someone to repeat a statement.

16 Quiet Time

Aim:	*To reflect on the theme or to introduce quiet times*
Ideal group size:	*Any*
Time needed:	*15 minutes*
Equipment needed:	*Bible, books, pens, paper*

Occasionally plan to spend part of your session as a quiet time, when the members (and leaders) of your group can be alone with God, to be silent. As well as being part of a group meeting, this is also a good idea if you are going away together.

Make it clear that for fifteen minutes or so, no one is to talk to anyone else. If individuals do not want to take part, that is all right, but they must not disturb others.

Give guidelines on how to spend the time. They could read a Bible passage relevant to your theme; read a meditation or a poem; pray; write something down. Alternatively, you could provide some structure, for example by reading something aloud, or playing a meditative song. If you have read something out, you could give everyone a copy of what was read to take away to think about.

You may think that this is impossible for your rowdy group. However, experience has often shown that it is not. It can provide vital space and time to think through issues raised in your teaching and in casual conversations. If we are not careful we find that we so overfill our programmes that no one has the chance to think.

4 Big Issues

Activities on relationships, Christian life and possessions

The ideas in this chapter explore some issues of particular concern to young people. They are just a selection of ideas, not a systematic approach to these themes, but they can help young people to apply what they are learning from the Bible to their own lives. They are also useful if you are planning a session which takes a thematic approach to one of these areas.

Relationships

1 Lover Lips

Aim:	*To start off a session on relationships*
Ideal group size:	*6+*
Time needed:	*5 minutes*
Equipment needed:	*Lipstick, tissue paper, Blu-Tack*

Get some small squares of paper (about half A5 size) and loads of lipsticks of the same colour (or use one lipstick and different applicators for each group member). Get each member of the group to put some lipstick on. Then they should all smack their lips on separate bits of tissue paper, in secret. Collect in the papers, and display them on the wall or floor. Let the group guess who they belong to.

2 What Happened Next?

Aim:	*To start a discussion on relationships or honesty*
Ideal group size:	*Any*
Time needed:	*15 minutes*
Equipment needed:	*None*

Read out the following to the group, or have some leaders act it out:

'Yvonne, a Christian, and Gary, a non-Christian, have been going out together for a month. Chris, who is a Christian friend of Gary's, has been trying to persuade them that it is wrong for them to carry on going out. Yvonne has been hiding the relationship from her parents, telling them that she has been going out with Chris. Gary has had a big argument with Chris which ended with Chris saying he was going off to talk to Yvonne's parents. What happened next?'

Get everyone to brainstorm their answers to that question. The idea is to come up with as many ideas as possible. You will need to emphasize that, while brainstorming, no one is allowed to comment on other people's suggestions. Afterwards, ask them to rate the different characters from 1 to 10 as to whether they were in the right or in the wrong. Lead into a discussion on relationships or honesty.

3 Soap

Aim:	*To introduce a discussion on relationships*
Ideal group size:	*Any*
Time needed:	*10 minutes*
Equipment needed:	*None*

The week before the meeting, assign each group member a soap opera to watch during the week, whether or not they usually watch it. Ask them each to watch out for the best moment, the worst moment and the most unbelievable event. Get people to report back on these, and use this to start a discussion about how those soap operas portray different relationships.

4 Liar of the Week

Aim:	*To start a discussion on honesty*
Ideal group size:	*4+*
Time needed:	*10-20 minutes*
Equipment needed:	*None*

Divide into groups of four. Give each group the task of talking about a subject of common interest, e.g. what happened at school last week. However, before they start, slips of paper are dealt out to them. On three of the slips are written the words: 'Talk truthfully about some things that happened at school last week – meanwhile see if you can spot who is lying!' On the fourth slip of paper is the instruction: 'Lie through your teeth about the things that happened at school last week – but be cunning about it! See how long you can go undetected, and how far you can go!'

After a few minutes, stop the conversation and see if each group has detected who is lying. Within each group, collect in the slips of paper, shuffle them, and re-deal them to the group. At the end of several rounds, the group can decide for themselves who they think is the best liar in their midst. At the end of the game, tell the members to resume their normal truthfulness, and give a prize of an elaborately wrapped empty box to the best liar.

Discuss the statement: 'There are sometimes good reasons for distorting the truth.'

5 Real Men Don't Eat Quiche!

Aim:	*To explore hurts and openness to others*
Ideal group size:	*Any*
Time needed:	*15 minutes*
Equipment needed:	*Assorted food*

This activity illustrates how we are all able, at different levels, to hide away our feelings, and to show how it does us no good in the long run. Select a mix of people for an eating contest. Be careful not to tell them what you are going to be eating! Invite them up front, and tell them that they must not show any pleasure or discomfort at what they are eating. Blindfold them and, first of all, try some trifle or other tasty pudding. Then something hot. Finally, serve up some extremely strong and spicy curry (vindaloo) or chilli, and watch the reaction. This could launch you into a variety of subjects and Bible passages.

6 Prejudice

Aim:	*To explore prejudice*
Ideal group size:	*6+*
Time needed:	*15 minutes*
Equipment needed:	*Large ball, blindfold*

This game is very good at getting people to feel what it is like to be frustrated and/or to be the object of prejudice because they are not one of the 'in' crowd. Blindfold one person and have the others stand in a circle around them. Have a large ball thrown from one to another across the circle while the blindfolded person tries to catch it. When *(if)* the person in the middle of the circle catches the ball, he or she can join the circle, and the last person who threw the ball is blindfolded and put in the middle.

As with most games like this, the effectiveness in teaching

depends very much on how you debrief people after the game. When you've settled everyone down, ask individuals how they felt, what made them feel excluded, what they would have liked to do about it. Give them time to think and answer. Spend time establishing what happened and what they were thinking about it, *before* you try to make any applications.

7 It's a Cop-out

Aim:	*To explore competition and ambition*
Ideal group size:	*4+*
Time needed:	*15-20 minutes*
Equipment needed:	*Short pieces of string, Mars bar*

Before the meeting, hide a Mars bar somewhere in the room. Have a large supply of short pieces of string (with slightly varying lengths) in a box. Tell the group that they have three minutes to make as long a chain as possible by tying pieces of string together. Immediately they finish tell them there is a Mars bar hidden somewhere in the room which can be kept by whoever finds it. When the Mars bar has been found, sit down and discuss the two games. How motivated were different people to win them? Was there anyone who did not really try? Did anyone compete more strongly in one game than the other? Why? Should Christians be competitive and should they have ambitions?

Lead into a study of Philippians 3:12-16 (you will need to look at verses 4-11 too). Are we 'striving to win the prize'? If not, why not? How can we?

8 Bam! Pow! Splat!

Aim:	*To explore violence and attitudes to it in the media*
Ideal group size:	*10+*
Time needed:	*30-45 minutes*
Equipment needed:	*String or masking tape, newspaper articles, cartoon words, marshmallows (lots!)*

This activity could be used for a session on the theme of war or violence, or could be included as a session when teaching Matthew 5, the Sermon on the Mount.

Before the group arrives, divide your meeting room in half with string or with a large piece of white masking tape on the floor. Decorate one side with violent pictures from newspaper or magazine articles. Decorate the other side with star-shaped cut-outs, reading 'BAM', 'POW', 'SPLAT' or 'OUCH', in true Batman cartoon style!

As the group arrives, assign them at random to different sides, either the cartoon side or the real-life side. Explain to them the two teams: 'Cartoon' and 'Real People'. Give each team a supply of marshmallows and explain that the goal is to get the other side out by hitting them with marshmallows, thrown underhand from your side of the line. Once you are 'out', you must lie down on the floor, 'dead'. The 'Real People' team have to be hit once to be out. The 'Cartoon' team have to be hit five times. Play the game for about 5-10 minutes, until one side has won. The

brave people can then eat the marshmallows!

Start the discussion: Was it a fair fight? If not, how did that affect the way you reacted/played the game? How do the media portray violence? How does that differ from the real world? How would you feel if the marshmallows were bullets? Is there a 'winner' in any war? Why or why not? Let this continue for about 15-20 minutes.

Then, put the whole group on one side of the line, and you stand on the other side of the line. Explain that you are going to play the marshmallow game again, but this time the teams are yourself versus the rest, and it will take ten marshmallows to get you out, but only one marshmallow to get any member of the other team out. On the word 'go', stand in place, without throwing any marshmallows, then fall to the ground when ten have hit you. Pause...

Break into groups of about five each. Set two or three questions like: How did you feel when I did not fight back? Is it always wrong to fight back?

Get the groups to look at the following Bible passages: Isaiah 2:1-4; Matthew 5:9-16; 5;38-39; 26:47-52; Romans 12:17-21; 13:1-7. Have each group discuss what they think the Bible says in each passage about violence and our reaction to it. Allow about twenty minutes for this.

Christian life in the world

9 It's a Dark, Dark World

Aim:	*To explore spiritual light and darkness*
Ideal group size:	*Any*
Time needed:	*20 minutes*
Equipment needed:	*Small lamps*

If you are going to have a discussion involving the values of the world, here's an illustration that might help. Close the curtains and use small lamps as the only lighting in the room. Collect a series of statistics and facts, relevant to your subject, that illustrate the point. As each one is read out, turn out a light, until you are in complete darkness. You may like to extend the discussion, looking at how we become used to the darkness, how we adapt to it, in order to get on: point out how it is like the world. Near the end of the discussion, abruptly turn on all the lights. It will make everybody squint for a while as it is too light, but should help to bring home the point about the effect of spiritual light in a dark world. Lead into discussion.

10 Pray Around the Country

Aim:	*To pray for the country*
Ideal group size:	*8+*
Time needed:	*10 minutes*
Equipment needed:	*Old road map*

Tear up an old road map and give a page to a number of small groups. Ask them to think of things to pray for based on that page. For example:

- farmers
- people who live in new towns
- road builders
- those who live in sparsely populated areas
- people who travel for a living
- places where land is being eroded by the sea
- people who always have to spell the name of their town or village when asked for their address over the phone
- anyone who lives in Basildon, for example.

Then pray together for those people and situations, imaginatively and creatively.

11 Practical Parable

Aim:	*To explore how we are to be ready for Jesus' return*
Ideal group size:	*9+*
Time needed:	*Several weeks*
Equipment needed:	*Money*

This idea leads into looking at Matthew 25:14-30, the parable of the three servants. It should be run over a number of weeks prior to the session on the above passage.

Split your group into three teams. Each team is a company. The members will be working together for a few weeks. Get them to choose a suitable name for themselves. Give each of the companies some money: £5 to one, £2 to another and £1 to the third. Say that they have a number of weeks to use the money to make more money (honestly!). Do not specify when you will be asking them to report back.

At a meeting a few weeks later, but without prior warning, get each company to report back. Discuss how their experience was similar to or different from the parable, especially with reference to the company that received only £1.

How did the companies feel about getting different amounts? Did they feel they were ready to give a report when they were asked to? Was it fair of you not to tell them when you would require them to report back?

Discuss what this parable was actually designed to teach – being ready for the unexpected return of Jesus by making the most of what God has given us at all times. Point out that this is one parable amongst four here in Matthew which teach about this subject.

12 What's in a Day?

Aim:	*To think about our relationship with God in everyday life*
Ideal group size:	*10+*
Time needed:	*10-15 minutes*
Equipment needed:	*Equipment for relay*

Divide the group into two or more teams for a 'typical-day relay'. Give each team a note pad, pen, magazine, aspirin bottle, diary, holdall, tie, coat and umbrella. Ask everybody to take their shoes off. The first person in each team has to put on the tie, coat and their shoes, pack the holdall, open the umbrella, and run to the other side of the room. Here they have to close the umbrella, take off the coat, empty the holdall, sign their name in the pad, put everything back in the holdall, put the coat back on, open the umbrella again and run back to the next person. They have to hand everything over and the process is repeated. Only try this in a medium or large sized room! You could adapt the items to fit with the lives of your group members.

When you have finished, get people to think back over their week and imagine a typical day. Ask them to remember how God has fitted into their lives during the week. Did he get much of a look in? Follow this with a short time of prayer focusing on thoughts that have arisen from the exercise.

13 Dressed Up

Aim:	*To explore outward appearances: clothes and Christian character*
Ideal group size:	*6+*
Time needed:	*15 minutes*
Equipment needed:	*Magazine pictures, paper, pens*

Have a fancy dress meeting. Allow every member one vote as to which is the most appropriate costume for the wearer. Have some magazine pictures of people in different clothes. Divide into small groups and give one picture to each group. They must write down as much as they think they can guess about the person from what they are wearing. Look at the fashions for Christians described in Colossians 3:12-14 and Romans 13:14.

14 Take Me to Your Leader

Aim:	*To explore Christian leadership*
Ideal group size:	*6+*
Time needed:	*30 minutes*
Equipment needed:	*Paper, pens*

Brainstorm the qualities required for leadership. In small groups write job adverts for the post of 'The Perfect Leader'. You will have to make it clear that you are talking about leadership in general, not just of your group or church. Have a panel to interview two or three members and leaders for the post, with the rest of the group as audience. Discuss the following questions: If Jesus had been an applicant would he have got the job on the qualities you listed? Which qualities that you listed would not come up to Jesus' standards? Look at Matthew 20:25-28.

15 What's My Line?

Aim:	*To explore what it means to be a Christian in different kinds of work and unemployment*
Ideal group size:	*Any*
Time needed:	*20-30 minutes*
Equipment needed:	*None*

Invite some members of the church in to play 'What's My Line?' Each one has to mime their occupation and then answer 'yes/no' to questions put to them by the group who are allowed fifteen questions to get to the right answer. You will have to make sure that the people you ask are not too well known to the group. If possible, include an unemployed church member, but be very sensitive to their feelings – they will in all probability feel very raw about not having a job and may be unwilling to join in this game. You could follow this with a more open question-and-answer-time on what it is like being a Christian at work, when unemployed, at college or at school.

16 Think Feel Do

Aim:	*To explore Christian responses to different circumstances*
Ideal group size:	*Any*
Time needed:	*10-20 minutes*
Equipment needed:	*Photocopied sheets*

Put at the top of a piece of paper the headings: 'What would you think?', 'What would you feel?' and 'What would you do?' Down the left-hand side write three or four different situations, for example: 'Meet a tiger in the High Street', 'Get ten Valentine's cards', 'Have your most precious possession stolen', 'Find £500 in the gutter', 'Discover you are going to have a serious operation', 'Your personal stereo packs up'. Produce enough copies for each member to have one.

Ask the group members to fill in what they would think, feel and do in each situation. Afterwards, discuss each one in turn. Ask what the group thinks a Christian should think, feel and do in the various circumstances. Which is the hardest to control: your thoughts, feelings or actions?

Money/possessions

17 World Banquet

Aim:	*To provoke discussion about the distribution of world resources*
Ideal group size:	*6+*
Time needed:	*60 minutes*
Equipment needed:	*Three types of meal*

People should come to the meeting without having eaten their evening meal. Explain that there are three sorts of meals in the world: about 29% of the world's population eat full-scale meals with large portions, plenty of meat and lots of vegetables; 33% eat sufficient meals, with mostly rice or wheat, no meat and only a few vegetables; and 38% eat inadequate meals, often with only a cup of watery soup or a small portion of rice with no meat or vegetables.

Randomly divide your group into three according to the percentages above and serve each the appropriate foods. When they have finished, ask each group how they felt about the meal. How did they feel about the other groups?

18 I'll Pay

Aim:	*To explore issues of wealth and need*
Ideal group size:	*5+*
Time needed:	*10 minutes*
Equipment needed:	*Character cards*

In groups of about five, give each member a card with a description of a character who might have good reason for being short of money. Then set the scene: 'You are in a fairly nice restaurant in the centre of town. You all came at the invitation of a mutual friend who did not turn up, but you decided to go ahead and start without him. Unfortunately, you have just finished the meal and he still has not arrived. The bill has come to £71.50. You have three minutes to justify why you should be the one who pays. When the time is up take a vote on who gets to pay – everyone must vote and you may not vote for yourself.'

Possible characters are:

- ❑ an unmarried student nurse
- ❑ a homeless person who has just found £71.50 in the street
- ❑ a single unemployed person living with parents
- ❑ a young manager, the only wage earner in a family with four children to support
- ❑ a pensioner, married but without any other family.

Add more information, including some local detail, to the character descriptions.

Discuss what made the vote go the way it did in each group. Lead into discussion of how we judge wealth and need. Who is poor? This could link to Bible passages such as the rich ruler meeting Jesus in Luke 18:18-30.

19 Noah's Ark Discs

Aim:	*To help group members think about their priorities and possessions*
Ideal group size:	*Any*
Time needed:	*10-20 minutes*
Equipment needed:	*None*

'You are a member of Noah's family. The weather forecast is not so good. It is going to rain for forty days and nights. There will be widespread flooding. Your home and city will be destroyed. Fortunately your father had the foresight to build an ark in the back yard. Only you and a few others will be allowed on board the ark. Naturally there is a space restriction. You may bring only three items. There will be an NIV (Nearly Inflatable Version) Bible and a copy of Graham Kendrick's Hits (Vols 1-15) already on the ark.'

Read, or give out printed copies of these instructions at the end of one of your meetings. Ask members to bring their three items along to the next meeting. At the meeting, depending on the size of your group, either stay together or split up into smaller groups. Ask people to show others in the group what they have brought and to explain why, out of everything they could have chosen, they have brought these items.

This should prompt an enthusiastic discussion about priorities.

20 Money, Money, Money

Aim:	*To explore attitudes to getting and having money*
Ideal group size:	*6+*
Time needed:	*20-30 minutes*
Equipment needed:	*Toy money, chocolate bar, poster-making equipment*

Plaster your meeting room with Monopoly (or other toy) money. It should be everywhere! Stick it under tables, on light shades, behind and under things. You'll also need to buy a very large bar of chocolate or something else appropriate to your group's tastes.

After the group has arrived explain that the plan is for them to collect as much money as possible, and whoever is the richest after five minutes can purchase the bar of chocolate. They can steal money as well as collecting it, but it must be whole, not ripped. After four or five minutes try to end the scrum and get them to sit down and count their winnings. Announce the winner, after adjudication, and present the prize.

Ask the winner how they feel about winning. Are they happy about it? Ask the whole group how they felt when they were fighting for money. How did they feel when someone stole money off them? Did they wish they had won? Is this game a fair representation of the rat race? How is it similar to or different from the way our society is organized?

Form groups of three or more, and give each group one of these Bible passages: Proverbs 11:28, Matthew 19:16-26, Acts 8:14-24 or James 5:1-6. When they have read their passage ask them to devise an advertising poster that depicts the message of their passage.

5 Group Builders

Ideas to build up group relationships

These are ideas which will help you to encourage good relationships in your group. Some will help group members to know each other better. Others can help them to pray and care for one another and to discover how to live as God's people together. A group of young people committed to each other, but also looking outwards, is dynamite.

1 Getting to Know You

Aim:	*To help group members get to know each other*
Ideal group size:	*Any*
Time needed:	*5-10 minutes*
Equipment needed:	*Your own item*

Ask each member of the group to bring an item to the next meeting which they can use to tell others in the group something about themselves. For example, this can be something related to their hobbies, to their past or to what they want to do in the future. Alternatively it could be 'the worst thing I own'. This is a non-threatening way of helping individuals to open themselves up to the rest of the group.

2 Crosswords

Aim:	*To help group members get to know each other*
Ideal group size:	*8+*
Time needed:	*10 minutes*
Equipment needed:	*Crossword grids, pens*

Give each person a piece of paper and get them to write down one thing about themselves that not many other people know (e.g. 'I won a 'bonny baby' competition when I was fourteen months old'). When this has been done, collect in all the bits of paper and use them to create a crossword puzzle with people's names as the answers to clues derived from the information that has been provided.

You could collect the facts one week, making sure you get some from those members who are away, to prepare the crossword for the following week. Alternatively, save the idea for a time when you are together for a while: on a weekend away, for example. When it is time to play the game, hand out pens and copies of the crossword. Let people mix freely, asking one another questions. (If you unexpectedly have someone new, get everyone to add their name to their crossword grids. While they are going round, they must ask that person for a fact they can write down as a clue, to go with their name.) The first person to finish the crossword wins.

3 The Wall

Aim:	*To build group identity, liven up the meeting room or introduce teaching*
Ideal group size:	*Any*
Time needed:	*3 minutes*
Equipment needed:	*Blu-Tack*

Ask everyone to contribute one item to put on the wall of the place where you meet. It can be anything at all, although you will have to make it clear that you have the right to refuse anything unsuitable. Either do it as a starter on a particular theme, e.g. ask everyone to bring something to do with prayer, or just use it to brighten up your meeting place.

4 Hi!

Aim:	*To welcome new people to the group*
Ideal group size:	*Any*
Time needed:	*10 minutes*
Equipment needed:	*Poster*

Get the group members and leaders to brainstorm ideas on how it feels to be new at something, and use their ideas to brainstorm ways of welcoming new people to your group. Follow the usual rules of brainstorming: come up with as many ideas as possible, however good or bad; all ideas are written down as they were said; no one may comment on the suggestions, they can just add more.

You could use their ideas to try acting out someone new arriving at your group. Do it twice: as the perfect welcome, and the nightmare welcome.

If it's not obvious where you meet and you are expecting some newcomers, you could have a sign outside saying something like 'Yes, you've made it, ... meets here!'

If you have a fairly large group, have two or three people, leaders and members, who will agree to welcome people as they arrive at your meetings. Give them some guidelines on what to do. For example:

- ❑ Make sure everyone is welcomed by one of the team. Don't just say hello but talk about at least one thing: what they have been doing in the week, what they are wearing, holidays.
- ❑ Introduce anyone new to at least one other person.
- ❑ Don't get distracted and just talk to your friends.

5 Wish You Were Here

Aim:	*To value each other more and to learn about the Holy Spirit*
Ideal group size:	*4+*
Time needed:	*15-25 minutes*
Equipment needed:	*Postcards, pens*

Give everyone a picture postcard of the area in which you live. Alternatively, use plain postcards. Ask them to write down on the postcard the name of one person they would like to have in the group, if they could. This could be a friend, a media personality, a religious leader, past or present, imaginary or real. They should write on the postcard 'Dear..., Wish you were here because...' When they have done this, jumble up the postcards so that everyone can read someone else's out. If there are any peculiar or outstanding choices give the person a chance to explain why they chose them.

Lead into a discussion using the following questions:

- ❑ Who is in the group at present? Do we really value each other? How could we be doing that more, and using the gifts we have as a group?
- ❑ Look at John 14:15-31 together. What difference does it make that, through the Holy Spirit, Jesus is with our group?

6 Round Here

Aim:	*To build up group identity and help members talk about their lives outside the group*
Ideal group size:	*Any*
Time needed:	*5-10 minutes*
Equipment needed:	*Map of local area, coloured pens*

Draw a large colourful map of your local area and get each member of the group to mark on it the place where they live. Mark the place where you meet. Then allow each member to choose one other place on the map to mark with a label. They may choose absolutely anywhere, e.g. the place I was born, the scene of my most embarrassing experience, the chip shop. Leave the map on the wall and, over the weeks, encourage group members to add to it any incidents that happen to them in different places.

7 ID Cards

Aim:	*To help group members get to know each other or as part of a session on identity*
Ideal group size:	*6+*
Time needed:	*5 minutes*
Equipment needed:	*Blank ID cards, Polaroid camera, tape measures and rulers, pens, string*

Prepare blank ID cards, with a space for a photo and, in place of the usual information, some strange details to fill in. For example: length of ear, longer foot, taste in clothes. If you can get hold of a Polaroid camera, take head and shoulders pictures of group members pulling weird faces as they arrive, and glue the photos on the cards. Then get the group members to fill them in, but with the rules that no one may fill in anything on their own card, and no one may fill in more than one answer on anyone else's card. Provide string so they can be hung around people's necks. You could lead into a discussion about identity and how we make judgements about someone from their outward appearance.

8 Gorilla Kidnap

Aim:	*To help younger teenagers transfer up to the youth group*
Ideal group size:	*Any*
Time needed:	*A whole meeting*
Equipment needed:	*Transport, gorilla costume, party stuff*

This idea was used by a group in Nottingham, to welcome younger teenagers who were due to transfer up to the youth group.

Contact all the parents of the new group members and arrange for them to be at home. Hire a gorilla costume, or improvise something similar, and drive round the neighbourhood knocking on the doors and gorilla-napping each person in turn. Then take them all off for a welcome party. The gorilla should take everyone home afterwards, if it hasn't turned into a pumpkin by then.

9 Programme Card

Aim:	*To inform the group about what is coming up and to build group identity*
Ideal group size:	*Any*
Time needed:	*Preparation only*
Equipment needed:	*Photocopier*

Many groups produce programme cards to show what they are planning for the next few months. Here are some ideas to make them work:

- ❑ Think up catchy titles for the meetings, which don't give too much away, but show that you have something good planned.
- ❑ Include leaders', and possibly members', names and addresses.
- ❑ Include any extra events and one or two whole church events which you particularly want to push.
- ❑ Make it funny. For example, assign each group member another person to draw a cartoon of. Use them all on the programme card.
- ❑ Make it look good. Some organizations produce cards with pre-printed artwork on to which you can duplicate or photocopy. For example, ask for sample copies from Christian Publicity Organization, Garcia Estate, Canterbury Road, Worthing, West Sussex, BN13 1BW (tel: 01903 64556). Alternatively drop in on your local instant print shop and see what they can offer you. For small numbers, photocopying on to coloured paper is hard to beat.

10 Listening

Aim:	*To help group members listen to and take notice of each other*
Ideal group size:	*6+*
Time needed:	*15-45 minutes*
Equipment needed:	*None*

Use this exercise to help the group members think about and improve their listening skills.

1. Organize into groups of three, and sit as indicated:

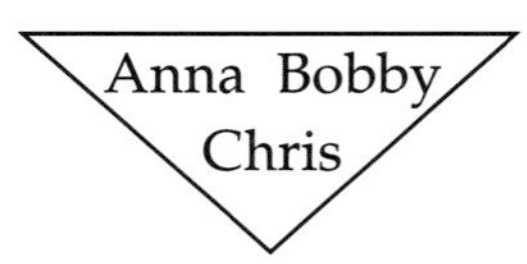

2. Anna talks to Bobby for three minutes on a subject relating to herself. Suitable subjects would be 'a funny or frightening incident in my life'; 'how I feel about God at the moment'; 'my average day', etc. Bobby is only allowed to ask questions, nod or grunt, etc! He is not allowed to give his own opinion.
3. After three minutes Bobby tells Anna what he remembers or understands of what she has said. Anna must not prompt or acknowledge what is being said.
4. Chris then indicates whether that was a reasonable summary, pointing out mistakes and omissions.
5. Anna then says briefly whether she felt Bobby was 'with her' most of the time, and what made her feel that way.
6. If you have time, change round. A becomes B; B becomes C; C becomes A. Repeat the exercise and then all change again, so that each person has a turn at each role.

11 Repair Kit

Aim:	*To encourage group members struggling away from home*
Ideal group size:	*Any*
Time needed:	*15 minutes*
Equipment needed:	*Suitable box*

If a group member has gone away to college or to work, and is struggling a bit, send them a personal repair kit from the group, to show your love and concern. It's no substitute for one-to-one pastoral work but, used in the right circumstances, it raises a smile. Work together on this, or get each person in the group to contribute one item, with a note explaining what it is for. Put them all in a suitable box (first aid or something similar). It might contain:

- ❑ a pen: to write a letter to share your problems
- ❑ a yo-yo: to bounce back
- ❑ a crazy golf ticket for two: to do something fun with a good friend
- ❑ some tissues
- ❑ a rubber: to start again
- ❑ McDonalds' vouchers: to go and pig out
- ❑ a paper bag: to blow up and pop when you need to let off steam.

12 Object Storming

Aim:	*To come up with new ideas to use in the group*
Ideal group size:	*Any*
Time needed:	*10 minutes*
Equipment needed:	*Paper, pens*

This is a sort of structured brainstorming. It can be used either in your leaders' meetings or in a group meeting, if appropriate.

Around the room, before the meeting, you should have placed various sheets of paper for people to write on. These sheets should be attached to a number of objects. For example, you could attach a piece of paper to the bin, the bookshelf, the wall, floor, cassette player, door, Bible, table, etc. Tell people that you are going to generate ideas (both new and old) to use in the group. Everyone should go round and write ideas on the pieces of paper. Each idea should be related to the object that the paper is attached to. So, ideas that use rubbish (or are rubbish!) should be written on the bin; ideas that use the Bible can be written on the Bible; if you meet in a church hall, way-out ideas can be written on a piece of paper attached to the exit sign, and so on. Encourage people to be imaginative by placing the pieces of paper in imaginative places. Use the ideas generated to start a discussion.

13 Best and Worst

Aim:	*To find out what the members like and dislike about the group*
Ideal group size:	*8+*
Time needed:	*10 minutes*
Equipment needed:	*Slips of paper, pens, rolled-up sock or ball*

Every now and then (but not too often!) it is useful to find out what people in the group think of what is being done. This activity will help you get a feel for what is liked, so that you can shape your future programme appropriately. However, it is worth noting that what people like is not necessarily what they need!

Everyone writes down secretly what they think are the best and worst aspects of the group's meetings. Get them to write the best on a slip of paper of one colour, and the worst on a different colour. Explain that these will be read out, but will be anonymous. Collect all the answers in a basket, then hand them out at random so each person has one of each colour: a 'best' and a 'worst'.

Throw a rolled-up sock, or a light ball around the group. When someone catches the ball they read out what is written on one of their pieces of paper before throwing the ball to someone else. Try to alternate between reading out 'best' and 'worst'. When they have read out a comment, they should place the piece of paper on the floor in front of them, so that everyone can see who still has things to read out.

It can be useful to write up summaries of what is being said on a flip-chart or overhead projector, listing what is said in two columns. Destroy the slips of paper. Lead into discussion by drawing out something general from the answers. Do not comment on the individual answers, which should remain anonymous.

14 Tape-O-Gram

Aim:	*To care for members who are away from the area*
Ideal group size:	*Any*
Time needed:	*15 minutes*
Equipment needed:	*Paper, pens, cassette player with microphone, blank audio cassettes*

Keep in touch with group members who have moved away from the area, or who are away temporarily at college.

Prepare a cassette to send to each person. On the cassette you can include messages from leaders and group members, news-flashes, audio-sketches, songs, etc. As well as being great fun to put together, these tapes are very encouraging to receive and can be a good way of supporting people, especially in the first term.

15 Where Have You Gone?

Aim:	*To keep in touch with group members*
Ideal group size:	*Any*
Time needed:	*5 minutes*
Equipment needed:	*Card, photograph, pen*

If you have been missing a member for a few weeks, raise a smile, laugh and maybe attendance by looking out a photo of them. The sillier the better. Stick the photo on to a postcard and at the start of your next meeting get the group to write little messages, or just sign it. Finish off by writing the date of the next meeting and signing it yourself. Post or hand deliver.

16 Gifted

Aim:	*To help group members think about their gifts*
Ideal group size:	*4+*
Time needed:	*10-20 minutes*
Equipment needed:	*Slips of paper with gifts on*

Prepare by writing on slips of paper lots of different gifts and qualities. You will need two slips of paper for each group member. You could use some of the following, but make sure that most of the gifts you include are things which might fit one or more of your group members:

- ❑ getting to know people
- ❑ artist
- ❑ doing practical jobs
- ❑ thinker
- ❑ carer
- ❑ being patient
- ❑ musician
- ❑ speaker
- ❑ having ideas
- ❑ dramatist
- ❑ reader
- ❑ understanding the Bible
- ❑ wise
- ❑ telling others about Jesus
- ❑ listener
- ❑ encourager
- ❑ pray-er
- ❑ teacher
- ❑ organizer
- ❑ giver.

Give out the slips at random so each person has two. Explain that the object of the game is to end up with two slips of paper which are gifts which could describe you. The way to do this is to swap slips of paper with other people. But this must be done in a set way. Both people must agree they want to swap a slip of paper, and then shake hands. Then they swap the slips, without knowing what the other person is giving them. They cannot swap with the same person again, until they have swapped with someone else. Carry on until quite a few of the group members have gifts they are happy with. Give everyone a chance to talk about why they are happy or unhappy with the slips of paper they have. Which were the gifts no one wanted?

You could repeat the exercise aiming to end up with gifts you would hate to have, or love to have. Use this to lead into more discussion about our attitudes to gifts. How much do we see them as status symbols, and how much as ways we can serve others? Lead into teaching from Romans 12, 1 Corinthians 12 or Ephesians 4.

6 Church Links

Activities to build up good relationships with the rest of the church

Young people need to build good relationships with others in the church, both for the sake of the church as a whole (including themselves) now, and to avoid being left like beached whales when they outgrow the youth group. The ideas in this chapter will help them to think about the church and their place in it; some involve other members of the church. With a little encouragement, you may find it is your young people who provide the energy to make them work.

1 25 Years On

Aim:	*To help group members relate to others in the church*
Ideal group size:	*3+*
Time needed:	*30-60 minutes*
Equipment needed:	*Paper, pens, present church magazine, photocopier*

Put together an edition of your church newsletter or magazine for a date twenty-five years in the future. Get members to work on different sections such as the minister's letter, news of church members, events diary, missionary news, adverts. Any references to present church members must be tactful, imaginative and hilarious. Some members could type or word-process the results and pictures could be added. You might decide to produce enough copies of the finished product to give to church members. This also works well as an activity to do with church members of different ages.

2 Perfect Mix

Aim:	*To start a session on the church or gifts and roles*
Ideal group size:	*4+*
Time needed:	*20 minutes*
Equipment needed:	*Cake-making equipment*

Ask each group member to bring one ingredient for a cake. The whole group should then make the cake at the start of the meeting. Bake the cake during the meeting. At the end, eat it. During the session have a discussion about what different people contribute to your church, or teach about gifts from Romans 12 or 1 Corinthians 12. You could make another cake leaving out something vital, to make the point that we all need it.

3 Magazine Special

Aim:	*To look at the strengths of your church*
Ideal group size:	*Any*
Time needed:	*45 minutes*
Equipment needed:	*Teenage magazine, blank front page of magazine*

Get hold of a copy of a teenage magazine, and photocopy the front page. Cut out the title and any other design features, and stick them on a blank sheet of paper, thus creating your own empty front page for the magazine. Photocopy the page, and give a copy to each member of the group, or work in pairs or threes. Ask them to imagine that the magazine is running a special feature on your church, looking at how good it is. They have asked your group to produce the words and plan a photo to go on the front cover. Show your group a copy of the teenage magazine to give them the idea.

You could also photocopy a blank front page on to an OHP acetate so that, at the end of the allotted time, you can put some of the ideas up on an OHP for all to see. If possible, get the results published in the church magazine.

4 Get It Together

Aim:	*To build up relationships with another group in the church*
Ideal group size:	*Any*
Time needed:	*A complete meeting*
Equipment needed:	*None*

Pick a group in the church that your teenagers have little contact with, for example the music group, a toddler group, the clergy or the church council. Arrange a suitable time during the summer for the two groups to get together for a joint activity. This could be a music evening, a sponsored knit, a trip to McDonald's. Plan something that will be active, so that people have something to talk about and can get to know each other.

5 You and Yours

Aim:	*To help the group explore their attitudes to the rest of the church*
Ideal group size:	*Any*
Time needed:	*10-15 minutes*
Equipment needed:	*Photocopied questionnaires, pens*

Give out this questionnaire and allow about five minutes for everyone to fill it in individually and privately. Then read out 1 Corinthians 13, which is about loving relationships in the church. As a group, think of positive contributions you can make to your church.

1. Choose which words describe our church and put a ring round them:
   respectable, fun, boring, friendly, cliquey, shrinking, happy, horrible, old-fashioned, enthusiastic, head-banging, small, amazing, ace, dead, growing, dull, super-spiritual, big, normal.
2. If you could change anything at all in our church, what would it be?
3. Write down every group you are involved in and all the activities and jobs you do within the church.
4. Which of these would stop you going to a church service?
   - ❑ an extra episode of my favourite TV programme
   - ❑ homework
   - ❑ an old-fashioned service
   - ❑ getting up too late
   - ❑ an animal rights rally
   - ❑ a date with a girl/boy
   - ❑ my best friend's birthday party
   - ❑ an earthquake
   - ❑ an international soccer match on TV
   - ❑ a family day out.
5. The best thing about our church is: ....
6. You are going on a church outing. Which member of the church would you least want to sit next to on the coach?

6 Excuses, Excuses

Aim:	*To challenge the group about involvement with the rest of the church*
Ideal group size:	*Any*
Time needed:	*20 minutes*
Equipment needed:	*Paper, pens, Bibles*

Split the group into teams and challenge them to list as many excuses as they can think of for not going to church services or getting involved in activities there. Have them read, and possibly act out, some of the best excuses. Vote for the best. Follow this by asking what excuses people give for not committing their lives to God. There may be some overlap, e.g. 'church is boring'.

Turn to the parable of the great banquet in Luke 14:15-23. What excuses are given here? They all suggest that those invited had better things to do. Point out that the parable is not about going to church, but about our response to God. Discuss whether commitment to church reflects Christian commitment. Or are they entirely separate issues? Be prepared to tackle questions raised over excuses for not committing our lives to God.

7 The Bare Essentials

Aim:	*To start a discussion about church services*
Ideal group size:	*4+*
Time needed:	*20 minutes*
Equipment needed:	*Item cards, large sheets of paper*

In this activity, members work in groups of four or five to decide what elements of a church service are essential.

To prepare, produce a set of fifteen 'item cards' for each small group. On each card or slip of paper, write one of the following: a minister; Graham Kendrick songs; Bible reading; confession; coffee; a sermon; prayer; music; drama; a leader; Communion; set prayers; a joke; hymns; a book review. If you have other regular elements in your church services, use those instead. Put each set of cards in an envelope.

For each group, you will also need a large sheet of paper with a line dividing it into two, and the two sides headed 'vital' and 'not vital'.

Get each group to sit around its large sheet of paper. Explain that no one may speak during this activity. The first group member then takes a card at random out of the envelope. That person must decide whether it is something vital for a church service, or not vital, and must put it on the appropriate side of the paper.

At each subsequent turn, a group member draws a card and places it in the same way, but may also choose one other card which has already been placed, and move it to the other side. No card may be placed on the line, but they may be moved back and forward as often as the players want. Continue until the last card has been placed. Then each person has one further chance to move just one card.

Discuss what happened, firstly in the small groups, and then all together. Use this to talk together about church services. What are they for, and what are the essential elements?

8 Kilroy

Aim:	*To get group members and other church members interacting*
Ideal group size:	*5+*
Time needed:	*3 minutes to set up*
Equipment needed:	*Large sheet of paper, Blu-Tack, pens*

Put a large sheet of paper on the wall, and ask everyone in the group to sign it. It is now their task to persuade as many people as possible from the church to sign their names on the sheet. This must be done by personal invitation only, not by having a notice read out in church. Try to get the signatures of everyone in the church in, say, two months. It will help group members talk to the rest of the church and, if you have a separate meeting place, get others in the church to visit it.

9 Prayer Pairs

Aim:	*To help group members and others in the church to pray for each other*
Ideal group size:	*Any*
Time needed:	*5 minutes to discuss*
Equipment needed:	*None*

Suggest to the group that they should each pray for someone of a different age group in the church, who will in turn pray for them. If you get enough encouraging responses from the group, approach suitable members of the congregation and ask them whether they would be prepared to take part. You should be flexible and allow people to choose who they pray for, if they so wish.

It would be sensible to talk to your church leadership about this before setting anything in motion. Encourage those involved to try to speak regularly to the person they are praying for, even if it is just to say 'hello'.

10 Church Visits

Aim:	*To find out about the wider church*
Ideal group size:	*Any*
Time needed:	*One summer*
Equipment needed:	*None*

Before the summer holidays, agree as a group that when anyone goes on holiday they must go to a local church on the Sunday (unless family pressure makes it impossible). They must then send a postcard to a pre-arranged address such as the leader's. They should also keep any church magazines or notice sheets they can. In September, when everyone has got back, have a meeting where you look at all the postcards, and those who visited churches report back. Ask questions to help them. Include information about the place where the church is situated. Then pray for each of the churches visited, especially any individuals who were met. Arrange the postcards and anything else they have brought back on the wall.

11 In Council

Aim:	*To raise awareness of what the church council does*
Ideal group size:	*6+*
Time needed:	*30-45 minutes*
Equipment needed:	*Church council agendas and minutes*

Hold a role-play of a church council meeting. Assign group members to some of the key positions – treasurer, secretary, guide leader, youth leader, music group leader, and so on. You could produce a card for each of these, with more information about the made-up characters. Give the council a budget of £400 to spend and a list of ideas for how they might spend it, such as the following:

- buy a second-hand piano (£200)
- mend the church roof. It is leaking but not badly. If you don't spend money now, it might get worse, or it might not (£350)
- refurbish the kitchen (£300)
- give a pay rise, in line with inflation, to the church cleaner and administrator (£100)
- pay for the youth group to decorate their room (£50)
- give some money to support an urgent appeal from an area of the world suffering from floods.

You could adapt the items to your own situation, but make sure that there are still difficult decisions to be made.

You could chair the meeting yourself, or get a group member to do this. But it is important that whoever is chairing encourages people to speak by asking specific questions of individuals ('Jane, what do you think of that?').

Afterwards, get group members out of their roles by asking everyone to say their real names. Then debrief thoroughly what it is like being on the council. You could get a group member to visit a meeting and report back, interview a council member or talk about some of the items which the actual church council has had to look at recently. This might lead to a group member being interested in standing for the council.

12 Look Back

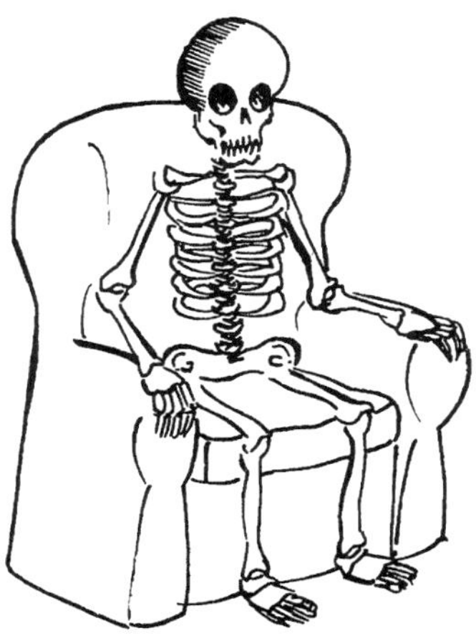

Aim:	*To find out about the history of your church*
Ideal group size:	*Any*
Equipment needed:	*Old church documents and photographs*

Pick a significant year in the life of your church. Give a presentation of what was happening in the world that year and what happened in the church. Invite along a church member or two who were around then and interview them briefly about how the church has changed, about what other things they were doing that year, and about how they became Christians. If you can, get hold of relevant documents and photographs from church life in the relevant year.

7 DATES AND TIMES

Ideas for seasons and occasions through the year

These are ideas to be used at specific times in the calendar or linked to particular events. Some groups have a set time each year when they break out and do something different. For others, a particular occasion or event can provide the inspiration for trying out something new. Or, if you're desperate, you can always think what you want to do and then invent an occasion to fit it.

1 A New Year's Resolution

Aim:	*To give a focus for the group at the start of the year*
Ideal group size:	*Any*
Time needed:	*5 minutes to set up*
Equipment needed:	*None*

Agree on a group New Year Resolution such as 'We will never say anything insulting, unkind or untrue about any other member of this group'. The group could also agree sanctions for anyone failing.

2 Navel Nite

Aim:	*To affirm everyone on Valentine's Day*
Ideal group size:	*Any*
Time needed:	*Whole evening*
Equipment needed:	*Invitations, clues for treasure hunt, photographs, envelopes, maps*

For 14 February, send every group member an anonymous card, with an invitation to a special Navel Nite event. Plan the event to be something which affirms all the group members, to relieve some of the Valentine's Day hype.

One possible activity is to do a treasure hunt around the local area in small groups. Plan a route which will look heart-shaped when drawn on a map. Take photographs of places around the route where you can put clues. The places need to be visually identifiable. Then at each point round the route, put the photograph of the next place to go to. It should be in an envelope with a word clue to the next place as well. Each group should have a map on which to draw their route. You could give each group a different clue to start off with so they start and end in different places. They finish when they get back to where they started with the map completed.

3 Christmas Charts

Aim:	*To use music to enjoy and celebrate Christmas*
Ideal group size:	*8+*
Time needed:	*45 minutes interspersed through the meeting*
Equipment needed:	*Cassette player, musicians, words of carols*

A week or two before Christmas, do a secret ballot amongst the group members, nominating 'the best Christmas music ever written'. Allow each person three choices, which they should write down. You could warn them a week beforehand, to give them a chance to think. Encourage them to think of all kinds of music: carols, pop music, classical or choral music, or anything else. Work out a Top Ten according to how many votes each one has received. In your session nearest to Christmas do a run-down of the chart, playing or singing each one as appropriate.

Intersperse the music with the other items of your programme: Bible readings, discussion, video, etc. You could include one or two interviews asking willing group members which pieces of music they chose, and why.

4 Active Vigil

Aim:	*To help the group to remember Jesus' death*
Ideal group size:	*Any*
Time needed:	*6 hours*
Equipment needed:	*Depends on activities planned*

Have a special meeting of your group on Good Friday from 9 a.m. until 3 p.m. – the time that Jesus spent on the cross. Plan a variety of activities which you will all do together, each one lasting half an hour. Then every hour, on the hour, stop to have a short Bible reading or to pray. Use these points to mark the time passing through the day. Some of the activities can be more serious, but some should be fun, too. Stick rigidly to the time allocated to each activity. Plan activities which will allow you to do that. One person could act as timekeeper.

The day will help to show that what Jesus did on the cross is not something separate from normal life. We need to remember it in all of our lives, not just when we are feeling particularly 'spiritual'. We remember Jesus' death not as people bereaved, but along with him, sharing the new life he has given us.

Here are some half-hour activities you could use:

- ❑ play the group's favourite game
- ❑ get one group member to teach the others a particular skill
- ❑ watch a video
- ❑ go for a walk
- ❑ work on a drama about Jesus' death
- ❑ provide a selection of books and magazines to read
- ❑ watch TV
- ❑ go to a local café for a drink
- ❑ make a Good Friday and Easter poster
- ❑ have a choice of smaller games (that can be stopped at any time)
- ❑ eat
- ❑ do some practical service – perhaps in your church building.

5 Light Show

Aim:	*To offer younger church members an alternative to Hallowe'en parties and to have fun*
Ideal group size:	*Any*
Time needed:	*Variable*
Equipment needed:	*Variable*

Many churches organize events for younger teenagers and children on 31 October, to give an alternative to Hallowe'en parties and traditions. This can be a brilliant opportunity to get older teenagers to take some responsibility for an event for younger members of the church. An early evening event based around the theme of 'God's light' works well. If the church does not already run this type of activity, get one or two of the leaders of the younger groups to help the group think through and plan a really good programme of drama, music, games, prayer and fun.

6 Scrap Book

Aim:	*To inform the rest of the church about the group*
Ideal group size:	*Any*
Time needed:	*30-90 minutes*
Equipment needed:	*Scrapbook, bits and pieces from the last year*

For the church Annual General Meeting, produce a scrap book of what has happened over the last year in the life of the group. You might include your programme cards, news sheets, members' photos, newspaper cuttings, events' brochures, link missionary letters, souvenirs, and so on. Alternatively, make an eye-catching poster.

7 Pollsters

Aim:	*To explore the link between politics and beliefs*
Ideal group size:	*Any*
Time needed:	*20-60 minutes*
Equipment needed:	*Photocopied questions*

Around the time of a local or national election, get the group to conduct a short poll with three questions:

1. Which one of the following problems facing Britain today concerns or worries you the most: burglary, violence, unemployment, housing, poverty, Manchester City's away record, AIDS, divorce, nuclear war, low moral standards?
2. Which one of the following do you consider the most desirable quality for a councillor (or MP or Prime Minister): high intelligence, honesty, attractive personality, beauty, authority, sincere Christian belief, wisdom, political experience?
3. Which party are you least likely to vote for at the election?

Try it on three groups of people: the youth group themselves, your church members, the wider public. They could also try it on friends at school. Compare the results for the various groups. Are there any big differences? Why? Use this to talk about how Christians are involved in politics.

8 Wind Down

Aim:	*To recover from exams and get back into Bible study and prayer*
Ideal group size:	*Any*
Time needed:	*A day or weekend*
Equipment needed:	*Camping equipment*

Young people who are involved in exams can find it difficult to make time for Bible study, prayer and time with the group. Help them to recover by having a 'wind-down' weekend for all the group after their exams are over. This could be for one day and night, or longer. If possible, go to an 'out of the way' location. You could camp in tents or use a youth or outdoor centre. Have a loosely structured programme which includes some Bible study and prayer, and some good group activities.

9 Festivals and Balloons

Aim:	*To help the group find out about some Christian heroes*
Ideal group size:	*6+*
Time needed:	*30 minutes*
Equipment needed:	*Church history reference books*

Three Christian festivals in the Anglican calendar for May are the death-dates of the following:

- 24th – John and Charles Wesley, priests, poets and teachers (1791, 1788)
- 25th – Venerable Bede, priest, monk of Jarrow (735)
- 26th – Augustine, first Archbishop of Canterbury (605)

Hold a balloon debate to decide which one of these festivals your group should celebrate. Introduce the idea of a balloon debate as follows:

'There are a number of people in a balloon that is fast losing height over the middle of the Atlantic. All attempts to regain altitude have failed: there are no more sandbags, the burner will burn no faster, the pet gerbil has been dumped. So, as a last resort, it is clear that someone will have to go! Each of the people in the balloon has to argue their case for why they should not be the one who is thrown out.'

Warn everyone about the debate a couple of weeks beforehand, and ask for four volunteers to play the above characters. Help them to research and prepare their cases. Each one needs to come up with at least three reasons why they should not be thrown out.

On the actual night, do the debate as a series of rounds, in which each person speaks once. The rest of the group then votes as to who is to be thrown out. Repeat the process with those who are left. After three rounds, you should have a winner.

10 Groupfest

Aim:	*To celebrate God's work in the group*
Ideal group size:	*Any*
Time needed:	*A whole meeting*
Equipment needed:	*Variable*

If your group does not already have an annual celebration each year, such as a group birthday, get your young people to create one. Have it at the time of year when your group members most need something to cheer them up: perhaps the middle of autumn. Get them to invent some suitable long-standing traditions, such as 'scroungemuggling' (visiting all the leaders' houses and demanding refreshment) or playing 'longkneeball' (sorry, the rules are secret). Three good elements to include are:

- to spend part of a session praising God for the life of the group over the last year
- a social event for the group members
- a slot in a main church service in which the group do something to show what has happened in the group's life in the last year. A sketch showing a typical group meeting (wildly exaggerated) can work well, provided care is taken that the jokes are not too 'in'.

11 Right Behind You

Aim:	*To support group members being baptized or confirmed*
Ideal group size:	*Any*
Time needed:	*5-10 minutes to show the video*
Equipment needed:	*Camcorder, VCR, video cassette*

If one or more of your group members is going to be baptized or confirmed, make sure you support them as a group. As well as doing a group card or present, or throwing a party to help them celebrate (why not have a water or hands theme?), also give them a chance to say something personal to the group about what they believe, and why they are taking this step.

One way to do this is to ask two or three group members to act as a video crew to make a video of 'a day in the life of...' They do not need to track them all day, but should have three or four pre-arranged times for shooting sections of the video. The crew need to be sensitive to the person who the video is about, and to remember that the aim is to affirm that individual, not to show off their own video skills. If necessary, a leader could be part of the crew. As well as showing that person in the places where they live, go to school and so on, the video crew should also be given the task of asking them, at some point in the day, to say a bit about what being a Christian means to them. Show the video at a group session.

12 Dish of the Day

Aim:	*To thank God for all he gives (at harvest or any other time)*
Ideal group size:	*Any*
Time needed:	*15 minutes to introduce*
Equipment needed:	*Paper, pens, photocopier*

For harvest, produce a recipe booklet with a difference to celebrate some of God's gifts to you as a group. Begin the process by asking the group to brainstorm things that God gives us. Use the list to get ideas for what might go in the booklet. As well as including some recipes to celebrate God's gift of food, think of other ideas which build particularly on the gifts of your group members. For example:

- ❑ a poem
- ❑ instructions for making something
- ❑ an account giving thanks to God for something that happened during the year
- ❑ jokes and cartoons
- ❑ information based on someone's particular hobby or interest
- ❑ a song written by a group member.

For some group members, their contribution might be to give thanks for the people they know. They might collect recipes, or other items from some of those people. Print copies of the booklet and sell them to raise money for Third World projects or something similar.

8 Extra Events

Special events to add something extra to the life of your group

These are ideas which will either take your whole regular meeting, or which can be planned to happen at a different time. A weekly programme with little variety of format can provide stability but it can also limit the ways in which young people learn and relate to each other. An occasional, very different event or activity can help them to learn new things, to grow together and to relate to each other and to you in new ways.

1 Canned Clubnight

Aim:	*To have a good time and get to know each other*
Ideal group size:	*6+*
Equipment needed:	*Equipment for cooking and eating*

A food evening with a difference! Get your members to invite their friends to this one – it is good fun and costs nothing. Send out two colours of invitation, one savoury, and one sweet. Those who get a savoury invite purchase a can of savoury food, remove the wrapper and hand it in on arrival. And those who get a sweet one bring a can of sweet food. Appoint some members and leaders to do the cooking. The only drawback is that you don't know the menu until your guests bring the food. Makes for some very interesting combinations!

2 Formal Dinners

Aim:	*To have a good evening and invite friends along*
Ideal group size:	*Any*
Equipment needed:	*Equipment for cooking and eating*

An increasing number of groups all over the country are having formal dinners. Most teenagers enjoy the opportunity to dress up well for a great night out with friends. These are great evangelistic opportunities. Why not invite some local Christian sports or pop person to be an after-dinner speaker? Don't be satisfied with a dusty church hall, try to get a nice home or other good venue. Convince the churchwardens to be waiters… go for it! You could even make it a canned formal dinner (see above).

3 Beach Party

Aim:	*To have fun and invite friends along*
Ideal group size:	*10+*
Equipment needed:	*Beach gear (beach not required)*

A great idea for summer is a mega beach party. (This idea came from a group who don't live anywhere near the coast!) Turn your church hall or meeting room into the beach. Use fake plants, sailboards, beach shades, Hawaiian cocktail bar, bouncy castle, water games, disco (the Beach Boys?). Let your imagination go wild. This is another cracking evangelistic opening.

4 That Was the Year

Aim:	*To have fun and get to know each other*
Ideal group size:	*8+*
Equipment needed:	*Music and items from the appropriate year*

Pick a year to give a theme to a party. Members can dress appropriately and you can dig out appropriate music from that particular year.

5 Record Breakers

Aim:	*To have fun and to get together with other groups*
Ideal group size:	*10+*
Equipment needed:	*Depends on choice of records*

Plan a day when your group, perhaps with others in the area, try to break as many bizarre records as possible. Well planned, this could be a great day out, with fun, food and teaching. This has endless possibilities: it could work well as an evangelistic fun day, or it could just be a good way to start your youth programme for the term. Why not ask local businesses to be involved, or get the police to judge the results... think creatively!

You could try to beat some of these records:

- ❑ most marshmallows stuffed into mouth (30 in one mouth)
- ❑ largest bowl of popcorn (13 feet in diameter)
- ❑ longest banana split (104 feet long)
- ❑ most peanut butter and jam sandwiches (1,000 made in 1 hour)
- ❑ most people on youth group couch (17 people)
- ❑ most people on toilet (6 people)
- ❑ most people in a Volkswagen beetle (20 people)
- ❑ most drinks cans in a van (3,292 cans and 478 2-litre bottles)
- ❑ longest litter pick up (200 consecutive hours)
- ❑ youth group cycle ride (454 miles in 50 hours – raising £2,500)
- ❑ most pennies together (1,000,000)
- ❑ smallest church (youth group meetings held in broom cupboard!)
- ❑ highest abseil (160 feet)
- ❑ remotest service project (12 hours by plane, 13 hours by bus, 6 hours by truck and 10 hours by boat, to build a new church in the Amazon! – the whole youth group went along).

6 This Is Your Life

Aim:	*To celebrate the work of a senior church member and to give the group a challenging project to work on*
Ideal group size:	*5+*
Equipment needed:	*None*

Stage a 'This is your Life' for one of your group leaders – possibly one who has been involved with the group for a number of years – or for an older church member or the minister. 'Fly in' old friends and group members at (not very) great expense. Dig up sordid facts out of their past! Get the group members to do the research and to plan and present the show. They will have great fun, will come into contact with different members of the church, and find out about the history of the group or church. Invite the rest of the church along to the show.

7 My Family and Other Animals

Aim:	*To draw in parents of group members*
Ideal group size:	*Any*
Equipment needed:	*None*

This was the title given to a 'parents' evening' run by the group at St Mary's, Reigate. A letter was sent to all the parents inviting them to the evening. A large number of parents and a few friends attended.

The purpose of the evening was initially two-fold:

- ❑ to explain to the Christian parents what the group was about, and to enlist their prayer support
- ❑ to present the gospel to non-Christian parents who would not normally come to church.

The evening also had an important side-effect in that it enthused the members of the group and, by taking part, made them feel part of a vibrant group.

The programme for the evening, which lasted an hour, included three sketches (two written specifically for the occasion), talks, interviews and singing. It also included an ex-member talking about the group – both when he was in it at its inception, twenty-five years ago, and now. It finished with a testimony from two of the leaders. Coffee and cakes were then served to the parents while they had the opportunity to look at photo displays and other memorabilia, and to enter a photo caption competition.

The evening was a great success and enjoyed by all who came. They strongly recommended it for other groups to try.

8 Staggered Supper

Aim:	*To have fun and to make contact with other church members*
Ideal group size:	*Any*
Equipment needed:	*None*

This is a popular idea that has worked well in many places. Different courses of a meal are served at different houses around the parish. Group members have to go from house to house to eat their meal. This requires the cooperation of parents and/or members of the church, and fairly careful timing on the night. It is good if the meals are held at the houses of adult members of the congregation since this will encourage better links between your group and the rest of the church.

If your group is too large for everyone to fit into a house at the same time, then you can send out smaller groups in different orders – so most groups will end up eating the courses in the wrong order. This always seems to go down well! The number of courses on offer will depend on how adventurous you are feeling. Five is probably the workable maximum (starter, main course, pudding, coffee, cheese and biscuits). You may want to charge people to cover the costs of those preparing the meals.

9 Sunrise

Aim:	*To break the routine*
Ideal group size:	*Any*
Equipment needed:	*Transport*

For the enthusiastic and the early risers! Instead of having your meeting at the usual time, you could try having it at odd times and in odd locations. Arrange to have the meeting early one morning as you watch the sun rise. This would be best done on a nearby hill or at a local beauty spot. If you do not have enough cars to take the group there, ask other members of the congregation, and get them involved too.

10 Camera Scavenger Hunt

Aim:	*To have fun and get to know each other better in small groups*
Ideal group size:	*6+*
Equipment needed:	*Cameras, film, lists of situations*

Divide your group into teams, with each team having a photographer with loaded camera, and an impartial supervisor-driver, briefed to drive safely. The aim is to accumulate points by taking photos of the team in situations of varying difficulty. Have the situations and points on a photocopied sheet for each team.

The following are suggestions:

❑ behind a wall with only heads showing	5 points
❑ in a telephone box	5 points
❑ behind a wall with only feet showing	10 points
❑ hanging from a tree (not by the neck)	10 points
❑ around a tombstone	10 points
❑ standing beside a particular roadsign	10 points
❑ in a bath, with clothes, without water	10 points
❑ in McDonald's, drinking a chocolate milkshake	10 points
❑ standing underneath a town clock at 8.30 p.m.	15 points
❑ standing on heads outside the church	15 points
❑ in a bath with clothes and water	20 points

If the photographers use slide film, then you can have a slide show at the next meeting. Alternatively, you can make a display of the photos and have an independent panel of experts award extra marks for artistic merit and pathetic stupidity.

Biblical Index

You can use the ideas in Know Ideas 2! *to teach a fantastic variety of passages, but the passages specifically mentioned are these:*

Time Required Index

Leaders' Preparation Index

This is a rough guide. You might be the fastest leader in the west.

Minimum Group Size Index

Watch out for activities that have a maximum group size if you have a larger group.

Subject Index